# Puratan Janam Sakhi

## Sri Guru Nanak Dev Ji

*Edited by*

# Bhai Sahib Bhai Vir Singh Ji

ENGLISH TRANSLATION

Front Page: Guru Nanak Ji with Mardana, C 1780-1800

ISBN: 978-1-09833-233-4

# DETAIL OF THE JANAM SAKHI.

The life-profile of Sri Guru Nanak Dev Ji is called the 'Janam Sakhi'. It has not yet been determined when the original 'Janam Sakhi' was written for the first time. Bale Wali 'Janam Sakhi' is considered by many to be the oldest. But a study of it has revealed that it may not be as old as it has been considered in the past. It appeared at the time of the tenth Master or a little thereafter. Bhai Mani Singh Wali Sakhi also cannot be older than the time of the tenth Master.

This Janam Sakhi, which is in your hands, has been considered by the learned ones, by virtue of its inner testimony, to be authentic, from the time of the sixth Master. (See the second quote at the end of the first Appendix). However, going ahead, we shall disclose that, in this Sakhi too, there appears a hint that it was written towards the time of the tenth Master. Any Sakhis that were written during the time of Guru Angad Dev Ji have not been discovered as of yet. It is an old tradition and it is apparent that the Hindalias wrote their own version of the Janam Sakhi after distorting the Real Janam Sakhi and gave it the name of 'Bhai Bale Wali Sakhi'. On going through that Sakhi, one comes to know that the Janam Sakhi of which we are giving details, was in possession of the writer. It is so because the lines and sentences of this Sakhi are found in the present 'Bale Wali Sakhi' and the third Udasi of Uttra Khan has been written literally by copying from this. It is quite possible that this manuscript is the genuine one; the original Janam Sakhi, from which the present Bale Wali Sakhi and other copies have been made from. It is also possible that there could be some other 'Janam Sakhi' out there and that may be the original one; more research needs to be conducted in this matter. Bhai Bale wali Sakhi in its present form, was written by the Hindalias after distorting this one or some other manuscript, which is not found anywhere. Hindalias, after distorting the two, wrote their own version, in order to eulogize Hindal and put him at a higher level. The fact becomes apparent after reading the Janam Sakhi of Baba Hindal.

The 'Janam Sakhi', which is in your hands, came in its modified form as Caulbrooke, after the name of an English gentleman who came across an old manuscript. He gave it to 'East India Company' and they kept it in the library of 'India Office London'. In 1883, the Sikhs of Amritsar made a request to the Lt. Governor that the 'Janam Sakhi' be procured from 'India Office London' for them to read. So, by virtue of the benignity of the Librarian Mr. Ross, the 'Sakhi' was sent to Punjab during the time of autumn harvest so that it could be scrutinized in the districts of Amritsar and Lahore.

On expression of an entreaty by the Sikhs to the Lt. Governor General desiring to have a photo copy of the manuscript, copies of the 'Sakhi' were officially printed through the process of Zincography and Sir Charles Atchison, Lt. Governor of Punjab, sent these as gifts to select places. After a short time, Singh Sabha Lahore got their own copy printed through Stone Press. It came to be known as 'Valait Wali Janam Sakhi'.

In a hand note written in 1885, Bhai Gurmukh Singh relates that he, during his tour, came across a 'Janam Sakhi' in Hafzabad and on its scrutiny, it proved to be similar to 'Valait Wali Janam Sakhi'; though there was scant difference in words, phrases and sentences. They named this one as 'Hafzabad Wali Sakhi'. This manuscript, as it appeared, reached Mr. McAuliffe. He, at his own expenses, had it printed in Gurmukhi letters, added punctuation marks to it and words were printed separately to make it readable. Its Preface was written by Professor Gurmukh Singh of Oriental College. That too was published through Stone Press in 1885 on 15Th November. That version of the Janam Sakhi came to be known as 'McAuliffe Wali Janam Sakhi'.

After that, Bhai Karm Singh, Historian saw a copy of 1790, deemed to be a manuscript of this 'Janam Sakhi' with pictures. It was in the possession of a book seller at Lahore. At the Janam-asthan Gurdwara, Lahore and at Ferozepur, he saw a manuscript of 1787 in which it was written that it was the copy of the 'Janam Sakhi' written in Burhanpur in 1727. He saw one copy in Hyderabad having been written in Shikarpur. He had seen another copy at the *dera* of Bandhais in the area of Bahawalpur. Mulak Raj Bhalla had seen one copy written of 1814 at Bardwan.

---

## A little scrutiny of the time of its writing.

(1) In the Sakhi of Guru Ji's Childhood Miracles (Sakhi 3), it is written that when 'Guru Nanak came of nine years; he was put to read Turkey – the Turk language.

When Baba Ji was at his childhood stage, it was the rule of Pathans and Persian taught in the schools. Turkey was the language of Turks or Mughals. People in common may be relating Turkey to Turkey or Persian or even Arabic; however, the status of Turkey as foreign language in every way could only be possible if the rule of Turks would have become permanent and considerable period of their rule had passed. As such, the Sakhi was written after the passage of a good portion of the Mughal period.

(2) This Sakhi contains *Sabads* of the fifth Master. As such, the Sakhi was written during or after the time of the fifth Master i.e. after the installation of Sri Guru Granth Sahib that was held in 1661 Bikrami (1604 AD). Considering its language and the words, many of the wise ones have deemed it correct to be the time of sixth Master.

(3) At the end lines of Sakhi 57, it is so written: 'Unforgettable is Guru Baba! Say all Waheguru! It is all Your protection'. The common use of 'Say *Waheguru*' had begun after the writing of Swayye by Bhatts. At first, *Waheguru* used to be a latent sentence in the semblance of *mantra* – a charm. It began to be used in general after the installation of Sri Guru Granth Sahib. This too takes us approximately near to the time of sixth Guru, but a sentence is there, in the text written above: 'Say all *Waheguru Ji ki Fateh!* The sentence '*Waheguru Ji Ki Fateh*' was given by Sri Guru Gobind Singh – the creator of Khalsa. The additional word '**hoeI**' takes us more towards the times of Sri Guru Gobind Singh Jee.

'*Waheguru Ji Ki Fateh*' – Victory of *Waheguru* – came in use at the time of savoring Amrit. That period was Bikrami Era 1756 i.e. 1699 AD. Under this reckoning, this Sakhi becomes correct after 1756 BE i.e., 1699 AD. It can be extrapolated that the 'Janam Sakhi' was an old one and the *Valaiti* manuscript may have been written after 1756 BE. The writer may have inadvertently written the prevalent sentence '*Waheguru Ji ki Fateh*'. It is also not possible that the text may have been written casually. But the researchers ought to devote their attention towards this point.

(4) Its language is not pure *pothohari* and neither is it pure of the south western undivided Punjab. It resembles the language of this or that bank of Jhelum. The use of letters 'h', 'u' and 'l' appear to be of obsolete use. The writer seems to be unfamiliar with the use of nasal hooks, though the same had acquired good shape in Amritsar and Lahore districts. The margin lines have not been drawn with a ruler, though the skill at that time was at its apex. The haphazard margin lines bear proof to the fact of scribbling in writing and as such, the writing too can be some sort of scribbling. The writer does not seem to be an expert or professional writer.

(5) The plea that the manuscript having reached 'Valait' bids to be the first and true manuscript gets rejected from its inner evidence. There was some other manuscript before this manuscript and it is a copy of that one. Then, is it the correct copy or some difference has come up? This becomes apparent after comparing it with the Hafzabadi manuscript that both the copies are from the same original one but are creating difference between each other. This makes a probability that the 'Valait Wala Manuscript' too must have undergone considerable changes from the truly original one. The fact that the manuscript pertains to be copy of some other one becomes evident as such:-

(6) In the Sakhi no. 28, it is written that 'he was a worldly *Faqir*,' The fore and after context relates that the text should have been: 'he was a religious-minded Faqir'. Since he laments that 'if he had asked for faith, he would have got faith. I desired for the world, and I got the world'. In Hafzabadi manuscript, the text is: 'He was religious-minded *Faqir*' and it is correct.

(A) This mistake of the *Valaiti* manuscript is such that it leaves no doubt about its shortcoming and this mistake is the argument of it being a copy. A correct reading of the Hafzabadi manuscript stands testimony to this argument.

(B) In Sakhi no. 30, Mardana's sentence is: 'Whatever be your sustenance, the same be mine. Do mine the same sustenance'. These words are superfluous. 'The same be mine' and 'the same be mine sustenance' depict the same meaning. One of them is needless. The real writer cannot do this mistake in his own manuscript. This is a mistake of copying; the Hafzabadi manuscript testifies this, wherein the text 'do mine the same sustenance' is not there.

(C)  In Sakhi no. 31, when Guru Ji concludes the *sabad* there is a factual error . In the Sakhi no. 30, the textual error.

(D)  In Sakhi no. 45, Guru Baba, there is a error during typing of shabad.

In the Hafzabadi manuscript, there is not so much of text after the Salok. The complete text was perhaps not in the original manuscript; or the copier of 'Valaiti' manuscript must have added himself the meaning of the Salok. If it be so, it has been missed by the Hafzabadi writer.

The final conclusion is that there was some other 'Janam Sakhi' before the 'Valait Wali Sakhi', though it was quite different. The 'Hafzabadi' and the 'Valaiti' may be the copies of some other Janam Sakhi and the truth as of yet has not been ascertained. These copies appear to have created difference from the original one.

———————————————————————

## Detail of what we have done in this work.

(1)  After making a comparison of the three: 1. Manuscript of the Photo of the Valait Wali Sakhi; 2. Stone Print manuscript of the Hafzabadi manuscript, which is popular as that of Mr. McAuliffe and 3. The manuscript of Stone Print of Singh Sabha Lahore, this copy has been prepared and all the differences denoting essential and meaning oriented expressions have been given in the foot-notes. Any of the differences considered unimportant have not been explained and the same text as in photo copy manuscript has been retained here.

The Sakhis that are in Hafzabadi manuscript and were not in Valaiti text have been included here in this and the same has been included in the note. If some text has been taken from there, it has been mentioned in the note.

(2)  Words have been separated by us and the marks like .., 1, ?

" etc have been put by us for facility in reading of the text. At places, we have put the dot (.) and the supra segmental symbol () so that the text may give correct understanding. Pages of Sri Guru Granth Sahib have been given by us.

(3)   Arrangement of the pages is of its own in publication of the book.

Pages of the photographed manuscript are given on the right page in line with old account books taking opposite pages as one page.

(4)   The Gurbani hymns have been given after correcting them in comparison with Sri Guru Granth Sahib, since the whetstone of Gurbani correction is based on Sri Guru Granth Sahib and any type of variant mistake is not acceptable.

(5)   If the Banis are not of the Gurus and have not been included in Sri Guru Granth Sahib and the outside Sakhi-writers have written those but the Gurus' names, their specimen has been given in the Appendix, and is not written in the book.

Sri Guru Arjan Dev Ji did not accept these Banis as Guru-creations and therefore, did not include those in the Bir. He called for the Pran Sangli from Sangladeep but was not accepted afterwards. Many of the Sadhus and Faqirs composed Bani of their own and tagged Guru's name to it. Out of many reasons, this too was one of the reasons for binding it in one Granth so that the practice could be curtailed. The clear meaning is that the practice of forty *yugas*, as said in the Jugawali, has been composed by some Saint; it is not by some Guru. It offers inner evidence that the Bani which has not been included in Sri Guru Granth Sahib and is in Sakhis or elsewhere per name of Guru Nanak was confirmed by Guru Arjan to be of someone else and therefore, was not accepted for inclusion in Sri Guru Granth Sahib. The life-period of Guru Arjan Dev Ji came about forty years after Guru Nanak. At that time, the entire Sikh faith, the elder Sikhs and the old writings were present with him, and any type of fresh checking of everything was not difficult for him by virtue of his intellectual proficiency. So he left aside the frivolous Bani that was not the Gurus' creation. So much so that whatever Bhai Banno had inserted in the second Bir, he expressed his displeasure over that also.

As such, the specimens of frivolous long writings have been given last in the Appendix, and the short Salokas have been left within. But it has been cleared in the notes given below that the text is not in Sri Guru Granth Sahib. It helps the readers to comprehend this clearly as what pertains to Gurus' compositions that have been included in Sri Guru Granth Sahib.

(6)    At the head of every Sakhi, we have given numbers as 1, 2, 3. ..

These are not there in original version. These are for convenience of the readers.

(7)    The addresses like Udasi First, Udasi Second that have been given in bold letters are given by us. In original version, no addresses have been mentioned after giving heading of the *Udasi*. However, the writing such as 'Third Udasi of Uttrakhand' in beginning of the Udasi is there in the original manuscript.

July-August 1926                                         Bhai Vir Singh

                                                              Amritsar.

---

## Translator's Note

Undertaking any service contributing towards remembering the Guru pertains to His Benevolence unto the seeker. The great privilege has been granted to me, genuinely in remembrance of Baba Nanak's 550th Birthday in 2019, by the Guru-lovers residing in USA. I took the work as if to propitiate the Guru, though it presented numerous knots to untangle in reference with language, particularly the Persian versions that Baba used in some of his discourses, comprehending at first and then translating into English the hymns not included in Sri Guru Granth Sahib, and then giving the version of foot notes at respective places in the form of Back Note References, for which I used my own discretion as it appeared convenient to present for use of the reader.

As a mark of acknowledgement, I must admit gratefully to have used translation work in English of Gurbani from the volumes attempted by renowned scholar Manmohan Singh Advocate, whereas my own humble attempt has been made to translate into English the Gurbani hymns not solicited in Sri Guru Granth Sahib. For this, I acknowledge to express my gratitude to Prof Jagdish Singh of Naad Pargas and S. Gursagar Singh of M/S Singh Brothers, Amritsar, though I did refer to *Mahan Kosh* of Kahn Singh Nabha and different dictionaries for Persian and Urdu languages also. For the translation in English of Vaaran

Bhai Gurdas Ji, I stand beholden to S. Shamsher Singh Puri for the purpose. These sources kept my buoyancy upheld while cruising through the project smoothly. Likewise, I stand beholden to Prof Ikwinder Singh (Computer Science Deptt) and Mm Gurpreet Kaur (Librarian) of Trai Shatabdi Guru Gobind Singh Khalsa College, Amritsar for providing me kelp in completing the project. In a way, all possible effort has been made to present a semblance of the original narration as it is in the *Janam Sakhi.*

While attempting the Gurbani versions, Gurmukhi digits have been used in expression of Gurbani hymns, but English digits have been used while attempting the translation in English.

I, by virtue of Guru's grace, feel beholden to Dr. Onkar Singh and Dr. Swarnjit Singh for affording me the privilege to undertake and attempt the project.

With Humble Submission,

Joginder Singh Jogi

Professor of English Studies(Retd.), Khalsa College Amritsar, India.

Jan, 2020

Email: jsjogi@yahoo.com

# SAKHI SRI BABE NANAK JI KI

*Sri Satguru Ji emerged to emancipate the world. In Kalyuga, Baba Nanak,*
*the Almighty Incarnate, took birth. By Grace of the Guru.*

## 1. Incarnation, Childhood

Baba Nanak was born in the year 1526 during the month of Vaisakh, (as per the Indian lunar calendar) in the third period of the moonlit night. His birth took place at the ambrosial hour when three fourths of the night had passed over and dawn was about to break. During this auspicious hour, it seemed as though the celestial notes were being chanted in the Lord's Court and thirty three crore gods professed obeisance to the divine nativity. It felt as though Sixty four female ascetics and fifty two stalwarts, six celibates, eighty four seers and nine abstemious beings tendered their homage to the blessed life that had embodied human form to emancipate the world. *"Do profess obeisance to him"*.

Baba Nanak was born to Kalu Khatri of Bedi caste who resided in the town of Talwandi Rae Bhoe Bhatti Ki. While growing up, he began to play with children of his village; however, unlike other juveniles of his age, he remained engrossed in meditation of the Lord. When Baba reached the age of five years, he started talking of the 'Being Inaccessible'. When he talked, he would be in full contemplation and present serious thoughts. The residents of the town were struck by his solemn views. Hindus deemed him to have been born as the God-incarnate; whereas, Muslims believed that he came to Earth as the faithful of the Lord Almighty.

## 2. *Patti,* the tablet; *Pandha,* the Hindu priest.

When Baba reached the age of seven, Kalu said: 'Nanak! It is time for you to study.' Kalu took his son to a *Pandha* to receive proper education. Kalu requested: 'O *Pandha!* You have to teach him.' Then the Pandha wrote on a *Patti*, the tablet for Nanak the alphabet consisting of 35 letters. Guru Nanak started reading the *Patti* in Rag Asa M: 1, in Bani form:

### *Rag Asa Mehla 1. Writing of the Tablet.*

### *There is but one God. By True Guru's grace, He is obtained.*

*S – The Lord who created the world, is the sole Master of all. Profitable becomes their advent into this world, whose mind remains attached to Lord's service.1. O man, O my foolish mind, why doest thou forget Him? When thou shalt adjust thy account, my brother, then alone thou shalt be deemed educated. 1.* **Pause.** *I: - The Primal Lord is the Giver and He alone is true. No account is left due from the Guruward, who understands the Lord through these letters. 2. U: -Sing thou the praise of Him, whose limit cannot be found. They, who perform service and practice truth, obtain the fruit. 3 N: -If anyone understands Divine Knowledge, he becomes a learned scholar. If anyone knows the One Lord amongst all the beings, he talks not of ego, then. 4. K: -When the hair grow grey, they shine without soap. Death-King's hunters come and they bind him with the chain of mammon. 5. Kh: -The Creator is the King of the world, who gives sustenance to man on enslaving him. Under His command, the entire world is bound and another's order prevails not. 6. G: -He who renounces the singing of Lord's Gurbani, becomes arrogant in his speech. The Lord, who has shaped the pots and made the world kiln, decides the time to put them therein. 7 Gh: -The attendant who performs Guru's service remains attached to Guru's hymns. He who deems bad and good as the same, He in this way gets absorbed in the Lord. 8 Ch:- He, who made the four Vedas, four production-sources, and the four ages, has Himself been in all the ages – the Renunciator, the reveler of the production-sources and the learned scholar. 9. Chh: -Spiritual Ignorance is diffused amidst all, and the doubt is Thine doing, O Lord. Having created doubt, Thou Thyself strayest the men and they, on whom is Thine grace, then the Guru meets. 10. J: -Thine beggarly men, who went a-begging in the eighty four lakhs of existence, beg for Thine gnosis, O Lord. The Only Lord takes away, and the one Lord gives. I have heard not of another second. 11. Jh: -Why die of anxiety, O mortal? What God has to give, that He continues to give. He gives, beholds, and issues orders according as the beings are to obtain sustenance. 12. N: -When I cast glance, I see not another. The One Lord pervades all the places, and the same One Lord dwells in the mind. 13. T: -Why practicest thou deceit, O mortal? Thou shalt get up and depart in* *a moment and trice. Lose not the play of life in gamble. Do thou run and fall under God's protection. 14. Th: -Comfort pervades the heart of those, whose minds are attached to God's Feet. The men whose minda are so attached, are saved, O Lord, and by Thine grace, they obtain happiness. 15. D: -Why makest thou ostentations, O mortal? Whatever exists, all that shall pass away. Serve Him, who is contained among all. Only then thou shalt obtain peace. 16. Dh: -The Lord Himself dismantles and builds and as it pleases Him, so doest He do. Creating the creation He beholds it. He issues commands, and emancipates him on whom He casts His merciful glance. 17. N: -He, within whose mind pervades the Lord, sings God's praise. He, whom the Creator unites with His own self, is not born again. 18. T: -Deep is the terrible ocean. The limit thereof cannot be found. I have no boat, nor any raft. I am drowning. Save me, O my Saviour King. 19. Th: -In spaces and inter-spaces, He, the Lord, is and by His doing, everything has come into being. What is doubt? What is called mammon? Whatever pleases Him, that is good. 20. D: -Impute not blame to any-one. The fault is of thy own deeds. Whatever I did, for that I have suffered. I blame no one else. 21. Dh: -Whose power has installed and upheld the earth and who has imparted dye to everything, whose gifts, everyone receives. His will works according to mortals' deeds. 22. N: -The Spouse ever enjoys pleasures but He is neither seen nor comprehended. Undoubtedly, I am called the wife, but my Groom has never met me, O my sister.23. P: -The Transcendent Lord, our King, has made the world to behold. He sees, understands and knows everything. Within and without, He is pervading. 24. Ph: -The whole world is entangled in a noose and bound with Death's chain. Only those persons are saved who, by Guru's grace, run and enter God's sanctuary. 25. B: -The Lord began to play the game by making the four ages His dice-cloth. He made all the men and other beings His draught-men and Himself began to throw the dice. 26. Bh: -They who search God and feel His fear, by Guru's grace, obtain the fruit. The self-willed fools wander about and remember not the Lord. They go round in the circuit of eighty four lakh of births. 27. M: -Because of worldly love, the mortal thinks of death and God, the lover of Nectar, only,, when he is about to die. As long as there is breath in the body, he reads of other things and forgets the letter 'M' (Maut, death), and God. 28. Y: -If man recognizes the True Lord, he is never born again. The Guruward utters, the Guruward understands, and the Guruward knows but one God. 29. R: -The Lord is contained among all the beings, which He has made. Having created the beings, He has put them all to work and they, on whom is His grace, remember His Name.*

*30. L: -He who put the creatures to various jobs has made love of wealth sweet to them. The Lord gives to eat and drink. Whatever befalls man under His will and command, he should endure it as alike. 31. W: -The All-pervading Lord is one Master, who created the vesture of the world to behold it. He (God) sees, tastes, and knows everything, and is pervading within and without. 32. R: -Why quarrelest thou, O mortal? Meditate thou on Him who is the Imperishable Lord. Meditate on Him, be absorbed in the True One, and be a sacrifice unto Him. 33. H: -There is no other Giver than He, who, on creating the creatures, gives them sustenance. Meditate on God's Name, be absorbed in God's Name, and night and day, derive thou the profit of God's Name. 34. A: -What God, who Himself made the world, has to do, that He continues to do. The Lord acts and causes others to act; He knows everything and like this, says Nanak, the poet. 35.1. (SGGS p 432-434)*

Thus Nanak studied for one day and remained silent the following day. Because he remained quiet, the *Pandha* asked him: 'Nanak! Why don't you study?' Guru Nanak said: 'I am through with all that is to study. I have gone through Vedas, Shastras and all other modes of addition, expenditure, daily money keeping and accounts; I have gone through this all.' Then Baba said: 'This learning is like tying a noose around our neck; it is superfluous.' Guru Nanak recited the *Sabad* in Siri Rag Mehal 1:

*Burn worldly love and pound it into ink and turn thy intelligence into superior paper. Make Lord's love thy pen, mind the scribe and write God's deliberation after consulting the Guru. Pen down the praises of God's Name and continuously write that He has no end and limit.1.O Brother! Learn how to write this account, so that where an account is called for, there thou mayest have a true mark.1. (SGGS 16)*

The Guru went on to say: 'O Pandit! Reading or listening is a humbug. Unless one recites the Lord's Name earnestly, everything is desolate.' Then the *Pandha* said: 'Nanak! Please inform me about additional knowledge; the learning that liberates one from this world.' Nanak said: 'Listen then, O master! This worldly knowledge is as such: ink is the lamp's soot and paper of jute and pen of the reed and mind is the writer and what is it that is written? All this writing is decrepit of wealth, it is fruitless. The writing that is truth is as follows: 'If the love of wealth is burnt to make ink and paper is made out of penance and whatever devotion is left after abstinence of desires, make a pen of that. The mind be transformed as a writer to write the Lord's Name. Write His praise as the writing may wipe off all flaws and falsehood. Write endless praise of the Lord as the writing may appease the body. The expanse of His endless limits can never be gauged.'

'O Pandit! If you have read this accountability, then teach me. If not, don't instruct me anymore. Listen, O Pandit! Wherever your soul goes, you shall have this *nissan* (the certification) of your reading and the god of death will never come near you.'

The Pandit said: 'Nanak! Where did you learn these profound lessons? But listen, O Nanak! What reward do they get who repeat the Lord's Name?' Then Guru Nanak recited the Second *Pauri*:

*The faces of those, in whose hearts is the True Name, are anointed with frontal marks there, where honours, everlasting bliss and eternal raptures are bestowed. 2. (SGGS 16)*

Guru Nanak said: 'Listen, O Pandit! Wherever shall your soul go, there shall be the reward of this repetition of the Lord's Name. This shall ever be attained in the form of ever-existent ecstasy and there shall always be available the treasures of day and night, the delight and delicacies; however, it shall be only for those who have meditated from the bottom of their heart and soul. Lord cannot be attained through any other means or by lip service.' On hearing this message, the Pandit felt bewildered and said: 'O Nanak! No one knows those who meditate on the Lord's Name, they don't get two square meals even for the day. And the ones who live like Kings, they do evils deeds and never recite His Name. How do I find what sins they have done who fear the King and fear not the Lord ever?' Then Guru Nanak recited the Third Pauri:-

*Some come, some get up and depart. They give themselves high names. Some are beggar born and some hold huge courts. By going into the yond, man shall realize that without the Name he is of no account.3. (SGGS 16)*

Guru Nanak said: 'Listen, O Pandit! Some come, some go, and the world is transitory. Some are rulers, while others are Emperors. Still there are many who have to beg for their livelihood. But, you listen, O Pandit! Those who shall go from here and have been enjoying without invoking the Lord, shall get punishment like a washer man beats the cloth on a stone or an oil-extractor who presses the sesame seeds. The sinners shall receive severe sores of hell. The ones who remember the Lord and eat by supplicating shall get honors in his Court.' Hearing this, the Pandit felt wonderstruck and murmured: 'He seems to be a great admirer of the Lord.' Later, the Pandit implored: 'Nanak! You speak with such profound wisdom, yet you are a mere child. Do enjoy the company of your parents, the pleasure of your wife along with the association of other family members as you have a long life ahead. On hearing this, Guru Nanak recited the Fourth Pauri:

*I am greatly afraid of Thine great awe, (O Lord!) and being distracted and bothered, my body is wasting away. They, who go by the names of kings and lords, are beheld being reduced to dust. Nanak, when the mortal arises and departs all the false affections are sundered.4.6.(SGGS 16)*

Guru Nanak then explained its subtle meaning:-

'Listen, O Pandit! Such is the fear of the Lord that my physical self has become anxious. Whoever has lived here and has called himself Khan or Sultan has perished and blended with the earth's dust. Those who had universal dictates, who were all powerful and due to whose influence, Earth felt tremors, have all died and perished from the face of this planet. Listen, O Pandit! With whom shall I have false attachment? Even I shall go away and shall disintegrate into the soil and merge with the dust. I shall remember the Lord who may receive this soul. Why should I have false attachment with this world?' The Pandit felt amazed on hearing such a profound message. He offered obeisance to the perfect one: 'Do whatever comes to your mind'. The Baba went home and sat down in silence. Everyone kindly utter you the Lord's Name, *Wahegur*!

# 3. Engagement & Marriage

As Baba grew older, he refrained from performing any type of work as per the Lord's resolution. Inertia prevailed and if he was sitting, he kept stationary or when asleep, he remained in slumber. He spent most of his time in the company of ascetics. Seeing his son's indolent lifestyle, Baba Kalu felt confused. He uttered: 'Nanak! If you remain like this, what will happen to your future?'

When Baba Nanak turned nine years of age, he was sent again to study Persian; however he decided to stay at home. He kept aloof and refrained from sharing his inner feelings with anyone. The well-wishers suggested to Kalu: 'Kalu! You should arrange his marriage.'

Upon hearing the advice of his fellow clansmen, Kalu contemplated on the suggestion and decided to get his son betrothed so that he could start his worldly life.

Soon after, the engagement1 took place at the house of Mula Khatri of caste *chona*.

When Baba attained the age of twelve years, he was married. Baba started working and performed worldly duties; however, his heart was attached to no one. He remained detached with other members of the household. His family would say: 'He strolls about these days with the faqirs.' Utter the Lord's Name, *Waheguru!*

# 4. The Green Field

As ordained by the Lord, Kalu, one day instructed Guru Nanak: 'We have these buffaloes at home. You better take them out and bring them back after they have consumed grass.' As per his father's order, Guru Nanak took the buffaloes out and brought them back after they satisfactorily ate pasture in the fields. He went the next day, left the buffaloes for their daily feed and slept at a comfortable spot located at the corner of his farm.

Meanwhile, the buffaloes went to the adjacent fields and started to feed in the neighbouring cover and devoured the standing crops. The owner of the land whose crops were consumed without permission was a Bhatti. He saw the buffaloes neglectfully grazing on his field as they were unattended.

The Bhatti got furious and in a rage said: 'O Boy! Your buffaloes have ruined my field and have consumed my standing crop. Why did you let this happen? How could this occur under your watch!' Guru Nanak replied: 'O Sir! Nothing of yours has been destroyed. Does it matter if some buffaloes had a mouthful of crop? The Lord shall send plenty to replenish your losses.' On hearing the words of Guru Nanak, the Bhatti got agitated and started to quarrel with him.

To remediate the dispute, Guru Nanak and the Bhatti went to see the head of the village whose name was Rai Bular. He remonstrated to Nanak: 'You are a careless person. You better call your father, Kalu.' As per the order, Kalu was summoned before Rai Bular, who asked him: 'Kalu! Why didn't you give proper instructions to your son? His carelessness has destroyed another person's crop. He is standing here and is furious. Rai Bular continued and told Kalu to compensate the owner for the loss of his crops or be brought before the Turks.' Kalu pleaded: 'What shall I do Sir? Nanak lives the life of an insane person.' Rai Bular said: 'I understand your plight and will excuse you as it is not an intentional fault of yours; however, you will have to pay the Bhatti for his losses.

Nanak was hurt due to this reprimand and refrained from eating or drinking for three months. Eventually, Guru Nanak told Bhatti: 'Go and look at your fields! Nothing has been destroyed there.' Bhatti replied: 'O Sir! My field has been wrecked. You must compensate me for this or I shall approach the Turks.' Guru Nanak said: 'Safe be all with you, O Dewan! If a single leaf be found plucked or broken, then inquest me; however, before that you must send your man over to inspect the crop.' Rai Bular asked his footman to report back from the farm. Wherever the person went, he found the crop standing intact. Not a single leaf was destroyed or disturbed in any way.

Then Baba recited the *sabad:-*

**Suhi Mehla 1.** *The renunciator practices renunciation and the glutton continues eating. He who is penitent practices penance and bathes and rubs himself at the pilgrim-places.1. I wish to hear Thine tiding, O Love, if someone sits and utters it to me. 1. Pause. As the man sows, so reaps he and whatever he earns, that he eats. Hereafter, no account is called from him, who goes thither with the Name's flag. 2. As are the deeds the mortal does, and so is he called. The breath, which is drawn without the Lord's meditation, that breath goes in vain. 3. If there be someone to purchase it, I shall sell, sell off this body of mine for my Lord. Nanak, of no avail is the body, which enshrines not the True Name. 4. (SGGS 730)*

The village chief, Rai Bular reprimanded the Bhatti and called him a liar for making false accusations against Nanak. Having been acquitted, Guru Nanak and Kalu felt gratified and went back to their home.

# 5. Shadow of the Tree did not Budge

As per the Lord's wish, two sons: Lakhmi Dass and Sri Chand were born in the house of Guru Nanak; however, in spite of having two healthy sons, Baba's dolefulness continued and he felt reclusive. Guru Nanak ventured into the woods as a dejected person. Baba one day went and slept in the garden. When the sun went up, the surroundings turned blazingly hot; however, the Baba didn't feel warm and remained in his slumber.

Rai Bular Bhatti was at that moment on a hunting excursion. While on the Chase, he came inside the garden, he found someone sleeping under a tree. He observed that shadow of the trees had gone to the other side; however, the shadow of one of them, under which Nanak was sleeping remained static and did not move with the altering of Sun's position. Rai Bular ordered his men to: 'Awaken him!' As he was forced to get up, Rai Buler recognized the person to be Kalu's son. Rai Bular spoke: 'O Friends! We had watched yesterday's incident and have observed this one also. It is not inconsequential.' Rai Bular Bhatti then went home and sent for Kalu and instructed him: 'Never rebuke or reprimand this child of yours. He is a person of God. My town sustains by his grace, Kalu! You must also feel thankful as I am gratified, in whose town he has taken birth.' Kalu replied: 'Only God knows His ways.' After taking leave from Rai Bular, he went home.

# 6. Agriculture; Business; Merchandise; Service

Guru Nanak started spending his time in the company of *Faqirs* and would hold regular discourses with them. He found immense satisfaction in the presence of their company and stayed aloof from worldly associations. Seeing this uncommon behaviour, Nanak's family members felt perturbed and concluded that: 'Nanak has gone deranged.' Concerned about her son, Nanak's mother advised him: 'You are unproductive by sitting amongst the *Faqirs* as they have given up worldly affairs. You have your household, wife, sons and extended family. You must engage in some kind of profession to support your family. You must leave aside this daily congregation with ascetics. People have started to deride us and are mocking us by saying that Kalu's son is indolent and does not earn a living.' The mother's censure had little effect on Guru Nanak and his thought process as he remained confined in his room for four days. When her gloom abated slightly, Baba's wife came to her mother-in-law and said: 'O mother-in-law? Why are you so indifferent? Your son has been lying inside for four days and he neither eats nor drinks anything.' Hearing the awful condition of her son, the mother came to Nanak and said: 'O son! Your inactivity is unproductive and is causing grief to everyone. You should eat and drink something. Do take care of your crops and fields. Please do start taking some responsibility and perform some sort of work. Your entire family is feeling disheartened. My son! Whatever you do not like, don't do it. We shall say nothing to you. Why are you feeling worried?'

Kalu came to know about Nanak's dismay and said: 'O son! What can we do for you? You have to start some sort of business which will be good for you. The Khatris' sons have money in the form of currency-notes and they do some sort of trade. To live in this world, you have to earn a living. O my son! Our crops are standing outside, ready to be harvested. You better not destroy them. If you will be helping out in the fields, people will say that Kalu's son is obedient and hard working. O son! Master's eyes make the crops flourish.' Guru Nanak replied: 'My dear father! We have taken care of a different crop and we keep it ever prospering. We have done the ploughing, sowed the seeds and fenced the fields. We keep a watch there all the eight quarters. O father! If we cannot take stock of our own crop, what shall we think of some alien's crop?' Kalu felt wonderstruck and said: 'Just see, O men! What does he say?' Kalu went on to remonstrate: 'When did you plough for a different crop? Leave aside these useless discourses and go ahead further. If you like, we shall prepare for you to plant a different crop next time.' Guru Nanak responded: 'O Father! We have ploughed the field as yet and the crop has prospered well. It is good to look and observe.' Kalu replied: 'O son! We have not seen your crop at all. What do you mean to imply?' Guru Nanak spoke: 'O respected father! The crop that we have ploughed, would you like to hear of it?' Then Baba Nanak recited the *sabad*:

**Rag Sorath Mehla 1 Ghar 1.** *Make thy mind the ploughman, good deeds the farming, modesty the water and thy body the field. Let Lord\s Name be thy seed, contentment thy earth-crusher and garb of humility they fence. Doing deeds of love, the seed shall germinate and flourishing, then thou shalt see such a home. 1. O sire, wealth goes not with the man. This mammon has bewitched the world and some rare person understands this.* **Pause. (SGGS 595)**

Then again Kalu spoke: 'O son! You can sit at our shop. We have our own outlet.' Then Guru Nanak recited the second Pauri:-

*Make the ever-decreasing age thy shop and make the Lord's True Name thy merchandise. Make understanding and meditation thy ware-house and in that ware-house, put thou the True Name. Have dealings with the Lord's dealers, and gaining the profit rejoice in thy mind.2. (SGGS 595)*

Kalu tried to reason by saying: 'O son! If you don't like to manage the shop, do work as a merchant, or as a horse trader. Without work, one appears and feels dejected; do undertake some sort of endeavor and explore other opportunities. We shall say that you have gone on a trading spree. Nanak shall return soon.' Then Guru Nanak recited the third *Pauri:-*

*Let the hearing of scriptures be thy trade and truth the horses thou takest to sell. Tie up merits for thy travelling expenses and in thy mind think thou not of tomorrow. When thou shalt arrive in the land of the Formless Lord, then, shalt thou obtain peace at His palace. 3. (SGGS 595)*

Kalu continued with his appeal by saying: 'Nanak! You have become misguided; however, you need to get involved in some sort of productive task. The storekeeper of Daulat Khan is your brother-in-law. He is a good businessman. You should go and work with Jai Ram. You may find that your interest may be aroused in another location. We have been deprived of your earnings. O son, if you go in a somber mood, the people will say that Kalu's son has turned out to be a *Faqir*; people will mock at us. On hearing his father's remonstration, Guru Nanak uttered the fourth *Pauri:-*

*Make the fixing of attention thy service and faith in the Name thy occupation. Make the restraint of sins thy effort and then alone shall people call thee blessed. Nanak, the Lord shall then look on thee with favour and thou shall be imbued with fourfold honour. 4.2. (SGGS 595)*

Baba addressed: 'Respected father! Listen to our sowed crop. O Father! Our sowed harvest has flourished well. We have ample support of this crop. It will redeem us of our debt to the Lord and no one will ask for anything more. Children will remain forever in comfort and the *Faqir* brethren will be blessed. The Lord, whose farming I have done, bestows his protection upon me. Since the day I have set myself in His path, I have remained blissful in mind and spirit. Whatever I ask, He gives. Dear Father! I have found such a Lord who has granted me all of the merchandise, employment and business opportunities.' Hearing this, Kalu felt confused, and said: 'O son! We have not heard or seen anything of your Lord.' Then Guru

Baba Nanak said: 'O my Respected Father! Those who have seen my Lord are all praise for Him.' Guru Nanak went on and recited another *Sabad*:-

**Rag Asa Mehla 1 Chaupdey Ghar 2.** *By hearing, everyone calls Thee great, O Lord. But one who has seen Thee knows how great Thou art. None can appraise and narrate Thee. Thine describers remain absorbed in Thee.1. O, my great Master of unfathomable depth, Thou art an ocean of excellence. None knows how much and how great Thy expanse is. 1. Pause. Meeting together, all the contemplators have practiced contemplation. All the appraisers having met together and have appraised Thy worth. The theologians, the visualizes and they who are the preachers of the preachers have described Thee. But, they cannot tell even an iota of Thine greatness.2. All truths, all austerities, all goodnesses, and the magnificence of the miraculous men, without Thee none has ever attained such powers. With Thine grace, they are procured. No one can obstruct and stop their flow.3. What can the helpless utterer do? Thine treasures are brimful with Thy praises. Why should he, whom Thou givest, think of some, other means? O Nanak, the True One Himself is the embellisher.4.1. (SGGS 348-349)*

Kalu repeated by saying: 'Relinquish these sermons and take up the common person's path. Without work, life is of little use.' Then again Baba Nanak remained silent. Finally, Kalu got up and went about his business. He said: 'He has gone astray from our work or dealings. But the crop never gets spoiled from outside.'

Nanak's mother came and instructed her son by saying: 'Leave aside the *Name* for a few days and rise up. Put on your clothes and wander about in the streets and in the residences so as to win people's confidence. Everyone may say that Kalu's son is a good person.' Baba replied to his mother by reciting the *Shabad*:

**Rag Asa Mehla 1.** *By repeating Thy Name I live. By forgetting it, I die. Difficult it is to repeat the True Name. If man feels appetite for the True Name, then, that appetite consumes his praise. True is the Lord and True is His Name. How can He, then, be forgotten, O my Mother?.1. Pause. Men have grown weary of recounting the greatness of the True Name, but have not been able to appraise even a jot of it. Were all men to meet and glorify Thee, Thou would grow neither greater nor lesser.2. That Lord dies not, nor is there any mourning (on that account). He continues to give and His provisions never run short. This alone is His merit that like Him none else is. There has been none, nor there shall be any.3.*

*As great as Thou art, O Lord, so great are Thine gifts. Thine is the personality, who makest the day and the night, too. Vile are they, who forget their Master. O Nanak, without God's Name, the mortals are outcaste wretches.4.2. (SGGS 349)*

After listening to her son, Nanak's mother got up and retired to her room. She informed the family of her plight. Hearing her dismal narration, the kith and kin of Bedis started to grieve and empathized with her. They said: 'Something strange and shameful has occurred at the residence of Kalu because his son has become deranged.'

# 7. Vaid – The Medical Practitioner

Baba Nanak stayed aloof for three months and deprived himself from eating or drinking anything. He detached himself from the outside world and stopped communicating with everyone. Concerned about this behaviour, members of the Bedi clan felt dismayed. They started saying: 'Kalu! How is it that you are unconcerned while your son is lying disconsolate? You must call a Vaid and take his advice for the treatment of your son. Who knows, once he is cured, he may be an accomplished person. Consider him to be a treasure, hidden under a straw, waiting to be discovered. As your son gets well, there shall be numerous sources of income.' Agreeing with his clansmen, Kalu arose and went away to call for a Vaid (the medical practitioner). The Vaid came to the house and took hold of Nanak's hand. He immediately pulled it back, shook his foot, got up, and said: 'O Vaid! What are you doing?' The Vaid replied: 'I am trying to check what type of ailment you are suffering from.' Baba laughed for a while, and recited the Saloka:-

*The physician is sent for to prescribe a remedy. Seizing my arm, he feels the pulse. (SGGS 1279)*

*Go home, O Vaid, and bother not my well-being. We being imbued with our Lord, who would you, give any medicine? (Not in SGGS)*

*O physician, being an able physician amongst physicians, thou first diagnose and find the malady, and then find out thou some medicament with which multitudes of maladies may be eradicated. (SGGS 1279)*

*On infliction of disease, the physician comes and stands with lot of medicament. Soul of the body calls the physician not to serve any medicine. Go your home, O physician, knowing little of anything. The Creator who has inflicted the disease, says Nanak, shall Himself rectify it. (Not in SGGS)*

Baba went on and recited one more *sabad* in relation to the Vaid in Rag

Malar Mehla 1.

*Firstly I feel the pain of separation from God and another pain is of the hunger for His meditation. Another pain is of the fear of strong attack of the death's myrmidon. Yet another pain is that infested with disease, my body shall pass away. O ignorant physician, minister thou not any medicine to me. 1. O simpleton physician, give thou me no medicaments. The pain persists and the body's suffering continues. Such a medicine produces no effect on me, O brother.1.Pause. Forgetting the Lord, man enjoys sexual pleasures, and then do the ailments arise in his body. The blind soul is punished. O ignorant physician, apply not thy cure to me. 2. The use of sandal-wood is the sandal's perfume. Man is useful as long as there is breath in his body. When breath departs, the body crumbles away. After that no one takes anything.3. Gold becomes the body and stainless the soul swan; in which there is even a particle of the Immaculate Name. All his pain and disease are dispelled. Through the True Name, O Nanak, he is delivered and released.4.2.7. (SGGS 1256)*

*Pain is arsenic and God's Name an antidote. Pound it thou in the mortar of contentment with the pestle of thine hand's gift. Ever, ever take thou this medicine and thy body shall pine not away. Otherwise death shall pommel thee at the final hour.1. O ignorant man, take thou such medicine, by eating which thou shalt be cured of thine sins.1. Pause. Empire, wealth and youth are shadows. Are the carriages, which are seen moving about in various places. Neither the body, nor renown, nor caste goes along with the mortal. There is day there, and here it is all night.2. Make thou relishes thy fire wood, avarice, thy clarified butter and lust and wrath thy oil. Collect them together and burn thou them with the fire of divine knowledge. Burnt offerings and sacred feasts and reading of the Puranas are, whatever is pleasing to Him that alone is acceptable.3. Arduous service of Thine, O Lord, is the paper and Thy Name, the prescription. They for whom this treasure of medicine is prescribed, look wealthy, when they reach the Lord's Home. Nanak blessed is the mother, who born them.4.3.8. (SGGS 1257)*

The Vaid felt alarmed, stood aside and said: 'O Brothers! Don't worry about anything. This person is the destroyer of all ailments.' Then Baba chanted another *sabad*:

*Rag Gauri M: 1. Of whom is the mother, of whom the father, and from which place have we come? From within fire and bubble of water are we sprung. For what purpose were we created?1. O, My Master! Who can know Thine merits? My demerits cannot be recounted.1. Pause. We saw the forms of numerous trees and plants, and many a time we were born as beasts. The man beats breaks into shops, strong palaces of coties, and stealing there from comes home. He looks in front of him, he looks behind him. But where can he hide himself from Thee?3. I have seen banks of sacred streams, the nine regions, shops, cities and market places. Taking the scale, the trader began to weigh his actions within his heart.4. My sins are as immeasurable as is the water with which seas and oceans are brim-filled. Show mercy, and extend a little pity and float me, the sinking stone.5. Man's soul is burning like fire, and the scissors is cutting his inner-self. Prays Nanak, if he recognizes Lord's order, then, day and night, he would have peace. 6.5.17. (SGGS 156)*

## 8. Preparing for Sultanpur

As per Lord Almighty's will, Baba Nanak came out of his confinement. Jai Ram was the brother-in-law of Guru Nanak and he worked as a treasurer at the office of Nawab Daulat Khan. He heard about the disheartening condition of Nanak who remained indifferent to the world and without any means of earning a living for his family.

He wrote a letter to Nanak and asked him to meet him so that he could help him out. Guru Nanak read the note and said: 'If I may be permitted, may I meet Jai Ram.' The members of the family replied: 'It shall be productive if you go there. He may even get you established in some sort of work.'

Guru Nanak decided to go to Sultanpur and left his house. On seeing Nanak leave, his wife became sorrowful and started weeping. While lamenting, she said: 'While here, you have seldom shown us any affection. When you will be gone, who will look after us, when will you return?' Baba replied: 'O innocent one! What was I doing here? And what shall I do there? I am of no use to you.' Then she entreated him again: 'As you were sitting at home, I took it as if the world's royal state was at home with me. This world is of no use for me now.'

Hearing her, the Guru became gracious and said: 'Don't worry about anything. You shall have day and night as your royal state.' Then his wife said: 'I shall not leave you and stay behind, please take me along with you.' Then Baba said: 'O Lord's being! Now I shall have to go. If my job fares well, I shall send for you. Please agree to this and take my word.' After listening to Nanak's assurance, she kept silent. Meanwhile, Guru Nanak's kith and kin saw him off and he proceeded towards Sultanpur. Say *Waheguru*!

# 9. Took charge of the Modi Khana

As was ordained by the Lord, the Baba reached Sultanpur. He met Jai Ram, and on seeing Nanak, he felt delighted. Jai Ram addressed his friends: 'O Brothers! Nanak is well.'

After exchanging greetings, Jai Ram went to the Khan's court and pleaded before Daulat Khan. He requested: 'All Greetings! O Nawab Sahib! My brother-in-law has come here and wishes to meet you.' Then Daulat Khan said: 'Go and bring him.' Jai Ram brought Guru Nanak with him in the presence of Daulat Khan. Nanak made an offering before the ruler. On seeing his respectful manners, Khan became pleased with him and asked: 'What is his name?' Jai Ram replied: 'He is called Nanak. Kindly assign him my job.' Guru Nanak stood there and appeared in a pleasing manner. Khan offered Nanak the robe of honour.

After appearing before the Khan, Guru Nanak and Jai Ram went home. Soon the Baba started working diligently; his work pleased everyone. The residents of the town loved Nanak and said that a 'blessed one' has come to live amongst them. The populace praised Nanak before the Khan, who was delighted with his new employee. Whatever surplus was left from his salary, Nanak disbursed it to charity in the name of God. Kirtan (singing of Lord's praise) was recited day and night. Soon after Nanak was united with Mardana, a Muslim bard. He came from Talwandi and settled with the Baba.

Nanak tried to help his fellow persons and whoever came to visit him was introduced to the Khan. He graciously allotted them the necessities of daily living and were provided work for their livelihood. The people were happy by the grace of Guru Nanak. Devotees would congregate at Baba's kitchen with reverence; they would routinely perform kirtan (sing Lord's praises) at night time. At the quarter of night, Baba would go to the river for his daily ritual bath. At dawn, he would take off his old clothes, change to new ones and anoint his forehead. He would then sit in his office and under court's order perform daily tasks required for his work.

# 10. Entry in the *Veieen*

The Veieen River flowed nearby and one day, as the Almighty willed, Guru Nanak took an attendant with him to the stream. There, he took off his clothes and gave them to his aide. Baba then proceeded towards the river to take his daily bath. As he immersed in the river and by the grace and consent of the Lord, heavenly courtiers took Nanak to the Almighty's Court. The courtiers entreated: 'O Lord! Nanak is present.' The Baba witnessed the True Court and the Lord became gracious and merciful. The attendant who accompanied Nanak to watch over his clothes felt concerned as he had been waiting for a while. He thought 'Nanak who went into the river has not come out of it as of yet.' He left and went over to the Khan and pleaded before him: 'I greet you, O Khan! Nanak went into the river and has not returned.' Concerned with this information, the Khan rode his horse and proceeded to the site near the river; he sent for his divers to search beneath the waters and had net barriers spread out to trap him. The divers searched the vicinity; however, Nanak was not found. Khan was concerned at not locating Nanak and became dismal with grief. He rode again and said: 'Nanak was a good minister.' Finally, after having searched tirelessly for him and not finding his whereabouts, the Khan went home.

As God willed, 'Nanak the devotee-incarnate was in Almighty's presence and was presented a bowl full of Amrit.' Order was given: 'Nanak! This Amrit is the bowl of my Name, you must drink it.' Guru Nanak obeyed the divine command and drank the bowl. The Divine felt gracious towards Nanak and said: 'I am with you. I have propitiated you and whoever repeats your Name, will receive My Blessings. Everyone has been informed of my will. You must proceed and repeat my Name and make the community also repeat thy true Name as it has been bestowed upon you. Always remain unattached with the world. Be ever engrossed in: Divine Name, Charity, Bath, Service and *Simran* (meditation). You must perform these tasks.' Guru Nanak offered his obeisance and stood up to leave. An order was issued and the command ushered: 'Nanak! How would you praise my Name? Say it.' Baba recited as the unstrung musical tone rose:-

**Siri Rag Mehla 1.**

*Were my age to be millions over millions of years; were I to have air as my drink and food, and were I to live in so narrow a place of a cave, where I may never see both the moon and the sun and where I would never have sleep even in dream. Even so I cannot appraise Thy worth. How great shall I call Thy Name?1. The True Formless Lord is in His own place. As I have often heard, I narrate the tale of Thine excellences. If it pleases Thee, induce Thy craving in me.1.* Pause. *Were I to be slashed and cut into pieces, over and over again, and put in a quern, and ground. Were I to be burnt with fire and mingled with ashes; even so I would not be able to assess Thy value. How great should I call Thy Name?2. Becoming a bird, were I to hover and soar through hundreds of heavens; and were I to vanish from every one's gaze and neither drink nor eat anything. Even so I cannot appraise Thy worth. How great shall I call Thy Name?3. Nanak, were I to have hundreds of thousands of maunds of paper; were ink never to fail me; were my pen to move with the velocity of wind in writing; and were I to embrace love for the Lord by reading and pursuing those writings. Even so, I cannot appraise Thy worth. How great shall I call Thy Name? 4.2. (SGGS 14)*

The Almighty spoke: 'Nanak! You have graced my Name, followed my order and whatever has taken place here, whoever hears the musicians and singers at my door will be blessed.' Then Baba spoke and a tune rose:-

*Rag Asa Mehla 1. Salok.*

*True in the prime; True in the beginning of ages; True is He even now and True He, verily, shall be, O Nanak!*

Soon after another command was ushered and the Order ensued: 'Nanak! On whomsoever your vision shall fall, they shall see my vision. On whosoever your grace shall be, my grace shall be upon them. My name is the Lord Almighty and your name the Guru Almighty.' Then Guru Nanak bowed at the feet and Baba received the robes of honour from the Lord. The *sabad's* melody rose as Rag Dhanasari took place with *Aarti* Mehla 1:-

*In the sky's salver, the sun and the moon are the lamps and the stars with their orbs are the studded pearls. The fragrance of sandal wood make Thy incense, wind Thy fan and all the vegetation Thy flowers, O Luminous Lord.1. What a beautiful worship with lamps is being performed? Such is Thine adoration, O Lord, the Destroyer of dread. The celestial strain is the sounding of temple drums.1. Pause. Thousands of Thine eyes, yet Thou hast no eye. Thousands are Thine forms, yet Thou hast not even one. Thousands are Thine holy feet, yet Thou hast not one foot. Thousands are Thine noses and yet Thou art without a nose.2. I am bewitched by these plays of Thine. Amongst all there is light and that light art Thou. By His Light, the light shines within all the souls. By Guru's teaching, the Divine light becomes manifest. Whatever pleases Him that is His real worship.3. My soul is bewitched by the honey of lotus-feet of God and, night and day, I am thirsty for them. Bless Nanak, the pied-cuckoo, with the Nectar of Thine mercy, so that he may have an abode in Thy Name, O Lord.4.1.7.9. (SGGS 663)*

The attendants were ordered: 'go and leave Nanak at the same place.' Guru Nanak, on the third day was brought out at the same landing place of the river. The people saw Nanak as he emerged out of the river. They exclaimed: 'O brothers! He had gone into the river. Where from has he come?' Guru Nanak came and entered his *dera*. He made preparations to close down his parish and instructed the gathering to take whatever they may please from there. The crowds, along with the Khan assembled there to see what was going on.

The Khan inquired: 'Nanak! What has happened to you?' The people replied: 'Sir! He was in the river for a while and has got injured.' The Khan thought: 'An unexplained phenomenon has taken place here.' Feeling helpless at the unrestrainable situation and his inability to help, the Khan was dismayed and left the place. At this time, Guru Nanak wore a single loin cloth as he kept nothing for himself. He went and sat beside the *Faqirs*. Along with him came Mardana, the menial who sat amongst the company of ascetics.

## 11. Discussion among *Qazis after* Namaz; Baba left the Treasurer Job

Guru Nanak remained silent the next day and on the following day, he declared: 'There is no Hindu and no Musalman.' He incessantly kept on repeating this message as ordained by the divine. When the community around the Baba heard these inconceivable words, they went to the Khan and remonstrated that 'Baba says: 'no one is Hindu and no one is Musalman.' When the Khan heard the citizens' concerns regarding the atypical statement, he re-assured them: 'Don't be concerned about it. He is a *Faqir*.'

While this was going on, a Qazi sitting nearby overheard the conversation and said: 'Khan Sir! It is strange what Nanak says: 'no one is Hindu and no one is Musalman.' In order to placate the Qazi, the Khan ordered his attendant to 'send for Nanak.' The employee went over to Nanak and delivered his master's message: 'Khan calls for you.' Guru Nanak replied: 'What do I care for your Khan?' On hearing Nanak's response, the crowd said: 'He has gone insane and delirious.' Guru Nanak heard the remonstrations of the community and said: 'Mardana! Set the *rabab* to play.' Mardana played Rag Maru on the *rabab* and Baba took up the *sabad-*

*Some say poor Nanak is a spirit. Some say that he is a demon and some call him a man. Ignorant Nanak has become mad after his Lord.1. Without God, I know not another.1. Pause. Then alone man is known to be insane, if he goes mad with the fear of God and recognizes none other than the One Lord.2. Then alone he is known to be insane, if he performs the One Lord's service and realizes his Lord's command. In what else is there wisdom?3. Then alone one is deemed insane, when he cherishes the love for One Lord and knows himself bad and rest of the world as good.4.7. (SGGS 991)*

After reciting the Sabad, Baba again became speechless. Whenever he spoke, he only reiterated: 'no one is Hindu and no one is Musalman.' The Qazi was unappeased and said: 'Khan Sir! He seems to be a rogue who repeats that 'no one is Hindu and no one is Musalman.'

The Khan again ordered his attendant and commanded him: 'Go and bring Nanak *Faqir* here.' The attendant obeyed the orders and went to Nanak's residence and said: 'Khan is calling you. Khan asks you to let them see your God. He wishes to see you.' Guru Nanak proceeded to meet him and said: 'Now I have received the call of my master; I shall go.' He put the cord round his neck, and advanced to meet him. On seeing Nanak, Khan said: 'Nanak! You are a friend of God. Take off your cord. Gird up your waist. You are a pious *Faqir.*' Guru Nanak removed the cord from his neck and girded up the waist. The Khan then asked: 'Nanak! It is seems that I am irrational by having a *Faqir* minister like you.' The Khan made Guru Nanak sit beside him and said: 'O Qazi! If you want to ask something, do ask. Otherwise, he will not talk again.' The Qazi laughed hesitatingly and said: 'Nanak! Why do you say that 'no one is Hindu and no one is Musalman.' How have you concluded that?' Guru Nanak recited the Saloka in Rag Majh:-

*To be called a Muslim is difficult. If one be really so, then he may get himself called a Muslim. First he ought to deem sweet the religion of the Lord's devotees and have his pride of pelf effaced as rasped with a scraper. Becoming the true disciple of the faith of the Prophet, let him put aside the illusion of death and life. He should heartily submit to the Lord's will, worship the Creator and efface his self-conceit. Therefore, if he is merciful to all the sentient beings, O Nanak! Then, alone he shall be called a Musalman.1. (SGGS 141)*

> **Salok M:1** *.Make mercy thy mosque, faith thy prayer-mat, what is just and lawful, thy Quran; modesty thy circumcision and civility thy fast. So shall thou be a Muslim. Make right conduct thy Mecca, truth thy spiritual guide and pious deeds thy creed and prayer. Rosary is that, what is pleasing to Him. Thus the Lord shall preserve thy honour, O Nanak!.1. M:1. Nanak, another's right is swine for him (the Musalman) and cow for him (the Hindu). The spiritual guide and the prophet shall stand surety only then, if man eats not carrion. By mere talk, man goes not to heaven. The deliverance is by the practice of truth, alone. By putting condiments in the unlawful food, it becomes not lawful. Nanak, from false talk only falsehood is obtained.2. M.1.. There are five prayers, five times for prayers, and the five have five names. The first is truthfulness, second the honest earning and the third charity in God's Name. The fourth is pure intent and mind, and the fifth the Lord's admiration and praise. Repeat thou the creed of good deeds, and then call thyself a Moslem. Nanak, all the liars shall obtain what is altogether false.3. (SGGS 140-141)*

After hearing the Baba recite this Saloka, the Qazi became wonderstruck. The Khan said: 'O Qazi! There is nothing left to ask him.

Soon it was time for Qazi's daily *Namaz* and everyone got up to offer their prayers and Baba also started following them. The Qazi stood ahead of all and started offering his prayers. While this was going on, the Baba started laughing at the Qazi. He felt offended when he saw Nanak smiling at him and thought that he was being mocked at.

After conclusion of the *Namaz*, the Qazi went over to the Khan and reported Nanak's impertinence by saying: 'Greetings unto you Khan Sahib. You saw the Hindu was making fun of us by laughing at Muslims while they were offering the Namaz and yet you say that Nanak is a pious person.' The Khan questioned: 'Nanak! Do you have an explanation to Qazi's accusation?' The Baba replied: 'O Khan! I care little of the Qazi; however, his *Namaz* has not been accepted. I laughed because of that.'

The Qazi said: 'If he has envisioned something, let him elaborate about my oversight.' Then Baba said: 'O Khan! When he was standing to offer *Namaz*, his mind was wandering somewhere else and his mind was diverted. His mare had delivered a calf and he had left the new born unattended, alone in his house. There is a well in the courtyard and he thought lest the young mare may fall into the well and get injured. His mind had been gravitated towards these thoughts and he was not concentrating on his prayers, therefore his *Namaz* has not been accepted.'

The Qazi heard Nanak's accurate explanation and fell at the Baba's feet. He said: 'Kudos! He has truly been gratified by God. The Qazi felt ashamed of his transgression, while the Baba recited the Saloka:-

*A Musalman effaces himself to acquire patience, contentment, pious creed and purity. Shall touch not the apparent and savour not the put forth. That Musalman, says Nanak, goes to paradise. (Not in SGGS)*

As the Baba delivered this Saloka, the Sayyad, Sheikhs, Qazi, Mufti, Khan, Khaneen, Mehar and Mukadam (*all Muslim religious officials*) felt bewildered. The Khan said: 'Qazi! Nanak has comprehended the Truth; there is no need to ask further.' Wherever Baba turned, he was greeted with love and devotion. The Baba chanted the following *Sabad*:-

## Siri Rag Mehla 1 Ghar 3.

*Make pious deeds thy farm, Guru's word do thou make the seed and ever irrigate with the water of truth. Become a husbandman and thy faith shall germinate. O fool! Know thus thy paradise and hell.1. Deem not that the Spouse is obtained by mere words. In the pride of wealth and the splendor of beauty, in this way thou hast lost thy life.1. Pause. The sin of the body is the puddle and this soul the frog, which values not at all the lotus-flower. Guru, the bumble-bee, ever repeats the Divine sermons but how can man understand them, when (God) does not make him understand. The preaching and listening of religious discourse is like the sough of wind for those,, whose soul is tinctured with mammon. Centering their attention on the Husband alone, those who meditate on Him, His grace descends on them and they become pleasing to His heart.3. Even though thou keepest thirty (fasts) and takest with the five comrades (i.e. five prayers) but beware, lest the one, who goes by the name of Satan should undo their merit. Says Nanak, thou hast to go the way (of death). What for hast thou amassed property and wealth?4.27. (SGGS 24)*

As Baba recited this *Sabad*, the Khan came and bowed at Baba's feet. Afterwards, the Hindu and Muslim members of the town came and spoke to the Khan and said: 'God speaks through Nanak.' The Khan ordained: 'Nanak! All of these treasures are yours, give your command and it will be obeyed.' Guru Nanak replied: 'God shall be gracious upon you. Now there is nothing else to talk about and all issues have been resolved. This royalty, these treasures and dwellings are all yours. I will leave from here and renounce them immediately.'

The Baba went over and sat amongst the *Faqirs*. They stood up reverently with hands folded and started praising him. They said that 'Nanak stands for Truth and is imbued in the hue of Truth.' Then Baba spoke: 'Mardana! Set the *rabab* to play.' Then Mardana played the *rabab*, and Baba took up the *Sabad* in Rag Tilang:-

## Tilang Mehla 1 Ghar 3.

*My beloved, this body cloth mercerized by worldly attachments, is dyed in greed. My beloved, such a cloak pleases not my Groom. How can the bride go to His couch?1. I am a sacrifice, O Beneficent Lord! I am a sacrifice unto Thee. I am a sacrifice unto those, who take Thy Name. They, who utter Thine Name, unto them, I am ever a sacrifice.1. Pause. If the body becomes the dyer's vat, the Name is put into it as madder and the Lord, the Dyer, Himself dyes, then, such a colour would appear, as has never been seen, O beloved.2. They, whose cloaks are thus dyed, O beloved, the Spouse is ever near them. O Lord, somehow bless Nanak with the dust of those persons. Serf Nanak makes this supplication.3. The Lord Himself creates, Himself stains and Himself He casts the merciful glance. Nanak, if the bride becomes pleasing to her Bridegroom, He enjoys her of His own accord.4.1.3. (SGGS 721-722)*

The *Faqirs* came over and kissed Guru Nanak's feet and received his blessings. Baba felt pleased with the *Faqirs*; he was thankful and gracious for being in their pious company. The Khan along with both Hindus and Muslims came to greet the Baba and everyone felt beatified in his presence. After spending time with the Baba, they took his leave. When the

Khan returned home, he was amazed to see the rooms in his house filled with treasures. Finally, the Baba felt contended and satisfied after the day's events and asked Mardana to walk along with him.

## 12. Made Mardana get Worshipped

Baba Nanak proceeded on his wanderings to remote destinations and refrained from entering any inhabited location. He traversed through the Jungles and crossed the rivers, yet he stopped nowhere to rest. Whenever Mardana felt hungry, Baba would inquire: 'Mardana! Do you crave for food?' Mardana would reply: 'You are omniscient, you know my inner thoughts'. Baba instructed Mardana: 'Go straight and stand at the house where an Uppal Khatri lives; wait over there and remain silent. They shall offer you something to eat Mardana! Any Hindu or Muslim who comes there shall greet you, shall bow at your feet. They shall put boundless dishes before you. Some shall offer you rupees, some shall place other worldly items before you. No one shall ask anything about you: where you are from or whose family you belong to. Whoever comes and greets you, shall say: 'May I place my entire self, unequivocally before you.' They shall say: 'We feel propitiated that we have had the honour of your glimpse.'

The Baba felt satisfied after explaining to Mardana and sent him to the city. While he was there, the inhabitants started worshipping him. As he proceeded, the entire city came to see him and bowed at his feet. As he wandered, he accumulated money. He bound the money and the gifts in a bundle of cloth and brought it back with him. Baba, saw Mardana with a huge bundle in his hand and started smiling at his demeanour. Mardana brought the accumulated items consisting of rupees and clothes to the Baba. Guru Nanak asked: 'Mardana! What have you brought?' He replied: 'O True Lord! By grace of your Name, the entire city came to see me and offered its respect and service. I decided to bring all of these gifts back to you.' Then Baba spoke: 'Mardana! You have brought back all of these accumulated gifts, you have done well; however, these are of no use to us.' Then Mardana said: 'O True Lord! What shall I do with them?' The Baba ordered: 'Throw these away.' Mardana threw away the bundle containing gifts. Afterwards, they both journeyed ahead. While walking, Mardana asked: 'O True Master! Whenever someone makes an offering by reciting your Name and feeds a devotee, does a part of that offering reach you? I am anxious to know this because you don't touch anything, nor do you consume anything, how do you remain satiated?' The Guru Baba said: 'Mardana! Play the *rabab*'. Mardana played the *rabab* and Baba recited the *sabad* in Rag Gauri Deepki Mehla 1:-

## Gauri Guareri Mehla 4.

*The mother loves to see her son eat. The fish loves to bathe in water. The True Guru loves to put food into the mouth of a disciple of the Guru.1. My beloved God! Cause me to meet such men of God, by meeting whom my sorrows may depart.1. Pause. As a cow shows love to her strayed calf on meeting it. As the bride shows affection to her husband when he returns home, so is God's slave immersed in affection, when he sings God's praises.2. A sparrow-hawk loves the rain water to fall in torrents, and the Master of men (King) loves to see the display of wealth. The Godly man loves to meditate on the Lord Formless.3. The mortal man loves to earn wealth and property. Guru's Sikh loves to meet and embrace his Guru. Serf Nanak loves to lick the feet of God's Saints.4.3.41. (SGGS 164)*

Mardana offered his salutations to Guru Nanak and they moved on with their journey.

# 13. Sajjan Thug

While journeying ahead, Baba Nanak and Mardana reached the abode of Sajjan Sheikh. His house was on the path they were travelling. Sajjan had built a temple for Hindus and a Mosque for Muslims in his home. If a Hindu or Muslim visited Sajjan, he would ask the guest to stay at his place and offered them food, shelter and hospitality. He would take care of his visitors and allowed them to offer prayers at their respective shrines. After looking after his guests, he would ask them to go to sleep at night. When his guests were in deep slumber, he would kill them by throwing them into his well. At dawn, he would again take up the guise of a saint and place a rosary in his hand and sit among the Muslims.

When Baba and Mardana arrived at his place, Sajjan offered them hospitality and made a remark to his followers: 'This man seems to be wise, knowledgeable and rich; however, it seems that he has concealed his money somewhere. He has radiance on his face, he is not deprived of any worldly possessions. Due to some vested interest, this man has become a Faqir.'

At night, after tending to his visitors, he requested them: 'Please go to sleep.' The Baba replied: 'Sajjna! We shall recite a *sabad* in praise of the Lord and then go to sleep.' Sajjan Sheikh said: 'All be well. Do recite it. Night is heading upon us.' The Baba said: 'Mardana! Play the *rabab*.' Mardana played Rag Suhi on the *rabab*. Guru Nanak delivered the Sabad Mehla 1.

## Rag Suhi Mehla 1 Ghar 6.

*Bronze is bright and shining but by rubbing it, its sable blackness appears. By washing its impurity is removed not, even though it be washed a hundred times. 1. They alone are the friends who travel with me as I go along and are seen standing there, where the account is called for.1. Pause. Houses, mansions and sky-scrappers, painted on all sides, when hollow from within, are like the crumbled and useless ruins.2. The herons arrayed in white feathers abide in place in places of pilgrimage. Tearing and rending they eat the living beings, so they are not called white. 3. My body is like the tree of bombax heptaphyllum. Beholding me, the mortals are mistaken. Its fruits serve no purpose. Its qualities my body possesses. 4. The blind man is carrying a heavyload and the mountainous journey is long. I see with my eyes, but find not the way. How can I ascend and cross the mountain?5. Without the Name, of what avail are other services, virtues and cleverness? O Nanak, contemplate thou the Lord's Name wherewith thou shalt be released from thy shackles. 6.1.3.. (SGGS 729).*

On hearing the Sabad and by the grace of Guru's presence, Sajjan experienced enlightenment and realized that he was in the company of a true saint. He introspected and became aware of his transgressions and said: 'I have committed numerous sins.' He then got up and bowed at

Baba's feet and kissed them. He said: 'Kindly forgive me for my misdeeds.'

The Baba said: 'Sheikh Sajjan! In the Lord's court sins can be pardoned in two ways.' Sheikh Sajjan asked: 'Kindly let me know how my offences may be pardoned.' On hearing this, the Guru became gracious and said: 'Speak the truth and confess that you have committed murders'. Sheikh Sajjan started acknowledging his crimes and said: 'I have committed evil.' Guru Nanak ordered: 'Give away the belongings of your victims to the needy.' Shaeikh Sajjan obeyed the Guru's order, brought out everything in his possession and donated it to charity in the Lord's Name. He started repeating 'Guru, Guru'. He became a devotee of Guru Nanak. The first Dharamsal (congregation site) was established Sajjan. Say *Waheguru!*

# 14. Discourse with Sheikh Serf

Baba Nanak and Mardana proceeded on their journey and reached Panipath. During that period, Sheikh Sarf was the Pir at Panipath and his disciple was Seikh Tatihar. He had come to fill a pitcher of water for the Pir. The Baba and Mardana were sitting close to the place where the well was located.

Seikh Tatihar came near the Guru, offered his obeisance and said: 'Greetings unto you, O holy men!' Guru Nanak replied: 'Greetings to the Formless, O Pir's disciple!' Hearing this, Sheikh Tatihar felt bewildered. He said: 'Up till now, no one has responded to a greeting in such a manner. I should inform my Master of this unusual salutation'.

Seikh Tatihar paid his respect to the Pir and requested: 'I felt surprised on hearing the voice of a holy man.' The Pir inquired: 'How does he appear?' Sheikh Tatihar said: 'Peace be with you, O Pir! I had gone to fill the pitcher. They were sitting close by and I offered my salutations to them. I said: 'Greetings unto you, O holy men!' Then he replied, and said: 'Greetings to the Formless, O Pir's disciple!' The Pir asked: 'O Child! Have you seen the one who greeted the Formless? If you have seen him, where are they now?'

Seikh Sarf went out and took Tatihar with him. He came to Guru Nanak, and spoke: 'If I ask you a question, O holy man! Please reply. How does this *khafni* suit you for separation?' Then Baba said:-

*The disciple unto the Pir remains intently dedicated. With khafni- long loose sleeveless gown - and cap, mind is to be kept ever engrossed in Word. Beside the flowing river, sits at the sand shore, and sitting calmly, one feels the comfort. Gaiety and gloom become the sustenance and by wearing the khafni, all evils are vanished, living becomes as tranquil as in benumbed state, and then is realized the artistery of khafni. Renouncing the family became single and then Nanak felt comfortable and at ease. (Not in SGGS)*

The Saeikh asked: 'Please reply to my question O holy man! Why do you just wear a sleek loin cloth?' Then Baba responded:

*Remaining tranquil and calm in grace of the Guru-Sabad, and keeping the heart ever stable among the five evils, one roams about ever in gleeful state. All the ten outlets be kept ever locked/suppressed with strict intent on the sixty eight pilgrimages. Wearing the loin-cloth, one perishes not thus remains single. With the lip tilted, one drinks pure water. Intellect exalted goes dwarf before the Guru, and this way Nanak wore the loin-cloth. (Not in SGGS)*

Again, the Seikh Serf asked: 'Please reply to my question O holy man. Why do you renounce your footwear?' The Baba responded:

*Swallowing all knowledge, day and night, within and through pure air are realized within mind all the sects. Living in the form of vegetation, on the earth and bearing in mind the cutting and shorning. Following the rite of standing at the river-bank side that fells as it wills, the efforts continue during churning. In this way, one sticks to the Lord's feet. Without realizing the Lord, if one renounces sticking to the Feet, says Nanak, the one sticks not to the roots. (Not in SGGS)*

Sarf asked: 'Please reply to my question O holy man!' Is a holy man's heart seen through his actions?' The Baba responded, and said:

'Mardana! Set the *rabab* to play! Mardana then played the *rabab*:-

**Being dead while living and sleeping while being awake and, knowing-well, one excruciates the self. Being all neat and tidy, one meets the people and then one calls oneself the dervish. 1. Is there someone a subservient with heart so dervish and having no gaiety or gloom nor hatred or anger and no lust? Pause. (He may) see gold like dust and recognize the true and false. (May) consider the coming salary deemec to be Sahib's and know not any other earning. He sits serene under the sky and plays the unstruck music. So is the eulogy of saints, says Nanak, and no Veda or Quran even know of it. (Not in SGGS )**

Sheikh Sarf said: 'Greatness to you, O Lord's bhagat! What more shall we seek from a True person like you! Your glimpse is enough.' He came near the Guru, paid his respect and kissed his feet. Afterwards, the Saeikh went back to his *dera*. Soon after, the Baba and Mardana left the place and proceeded further with their travels.

# 15. In Delhi, a Dead Elephant Re-Enlivened

After travelling for a while, Guru Nanak and Mardana reached Delhi. 1Brahm Beg was its King at that time. Once in Delhi, Guru Nanak stayed with a *mahout* (the elephant-keeper) who offered them his sincere and earnest service.

While residing there, they found a dead elephant nearby. People were wailing and crying at the sight of the departed animal. Baba asked: 'Why are you weeping?' They entreated: 'We are weeping because of the dead elephant.' The Baba asked: 'Who did the elephant belong to?' The *Mahout* said: 'It belonged to the King; it was of the Lord.' The Baba said: 'Why are you weeping?' They said: 'It was our source of earning, our livelihood.' The Baba told them: 'Do some other type of work.' Then they said: 'O Baba! It was an established and smooth-running business. Families were living well'. The Baba became gracious. He said: 'If the elephant becomes alive, will you stop weeping?' They said: 'How can the dead become alive again?' The Baba said: 'Go and roll your hand on its mouth, and say *Waheguru*'! They obeyed, rolled their hand on the mouth, and the elephant stood up.

The King was informed of this miracle and he asked for the elephant to be sent to him. He rode over to have a glimpse of Guru Nanak and sat nearby. He said: 'O holy man! Is it you who has made the elephant re-live?' The Baba replied: 'Lord only makes one live or die. *Faqirs* offer entreaty only and the Lord becomes gracious.' The king said: 'Make the elephant dead again'. Then Baba spoke:-

**Salok.** *He only causes to live and die. None else is there, says Nanak, but the One.(Not in SGGS)* .

Soon after, the elephant died. The king ordered: 'Make it relive.' The Baba said: 'Reverend! Iron becomes red hot when put in fire. But it cannot be placed on one's hand for a while, until it has cooled down. And a live coal can't be placed on one's hand for a long duration. *Faqirs* have been red hot in hue of the Lord and they can bear with the Lord's heat, but their own heat is difficult to bear.' Getting a hint of the mystic message, the king became pleased. He said: 'Do accept something, O reverent'! Then Baba spoke:-

**Salok.** *Nanak has hunger of God; else is carefreeness. We crave for the Vision only; no other desire is there. (Not in SGGS)*

Having understood the profound and divine message, the king got up and took leave of the Guru. Having spent some time in Delhi, the Baba proceeded further with his journey.

# FIRST TRAVELOGUE – the First *Udasi*

## 16. Apparel during the First Travelogue

**Sheikh Bajid:**

By divine will of the Guru gracious! First travelogue of Guru Nanak was undertaken towards the East. Mardana *rababi* also accompanied Baba Nanak on his Travelogue. During their travels, food was scarcely available, therefore their diet consisted of air and water for sustenance. The robes worn by the Baba were: a dress of unripen mango green colour and the other was white. He put a shoe on one foot and a 1wooden sandal on the other; one *khafni* (long loose sleeveless gown); a Mohammadan monk's hat (*kalandri*); a rosary of bones around his neck and his forehead was anointed with saffron.

While they were travelling, they met Seikh Bajid Sayyad who was riding in a palanquin, which was being carried by six pall-bearers. After a while, the palanquin was brought to rest under a tree that was casting a shade from the bright sun. Seikh Bajid Sayyad's attendants subsequently attended to their master and massaged his body and were waving a fan upon him. Seeing this, Mardana asked: 'Are there many Lords and Why?' Then Baba replied: 'Mardana! God is One.' Then Mardana inquired further: 'Yes, Master! Whose creation are the attendants and whose creation is he who has come riding in the palanquin? The servants are bare-foot with bare back; they have woolen covers on naked shoulders. They are serving and massaging the body of the Sayyad who is relaxing.' The Baba spoke:-

*Recluse of the prior birth have borne the chill-sting. Being tired of the time are getting massaged the limbs now. (Not in SGGS)*

The Baba explained: 'Mardana! One finds regality after penance; hell after the rule. Whoever has come, has come naked from his mother's belly. The pleasure and pain from past life's account is brought forward to the next life. One is rewarded for his good deeds and has to pay for his sins.' Mardana understood the Guru's message and bowed at his feet.

# 17. Chatur Dass in Benaras

While proceeding on their journey, Guru Nanak and Mardana reached the city of Benaras whose Pandit was Chatur Das. After entering the holy city, they sat in a kitchen. Shortly afterwards, the Pandit came for his bath and offered greetings to the Guru. Seeing Baba's distinctive robes, the Pandit sat down, and inquired: 'You don't have the *Saligram* (the worshipping stone), no rosary of *Tulsi* (basil), no anointment of sandalwood and you call yourself a *Bhagat*. So what sort of *bhagti* (the religious observance) have you acquired?' The Baba said: 'Mardana! Play the *rabab*'. Mardana played the *rabab*, and tuned it to *Rag Basant*. Baba recited the *Sabad*:-

## Mehla 1 Basant Hindole Ghar 2.

*O Brahaman, thou worshippest and propitiate the stone-god and deemest it a good act to wear the rosary of sweet basil. Build thou the boat of the meditation of the Lord's Name and pray, "O Merciful Master! Take Thou pity on me." 1. Why irrigate thou the field of saltpeter and thus wastest thy human life? The wall of mud shall surely fall. Why plasterest it thou with lime?* **Pause.**

After hearing the Sabad, the Pandit asked: 'O Bhagat! Soil may be tilled, but how can it prosper without irrigation? How can the gardener do all of this on his own?' Then Baba recited the second stanza:- *Make God thy well, string to its chain the buckets of His Name and yoke thy mind as an ox thereto. Irrigate, thou with Nectar and fill the small plots therewith. Then shalt thou belong to the Gardener.2.*

The Pandit enquired further by asking: 'O Bhagat! This is the way to irrigate barren land; however, please explain the process that helps irrigate the entire Earth? And how may one acquire the Lord'? Then Baba recited the third Stanza:-

*Make both lust and wrath thy hand-hoes and therewith loosen thy farm, O brother. The more thou hoest, the more the peace, thou shalt obtain. The deeds done can be effaced not. 3.*

Then Pandit Chatur Das asked: 'O Great One! You are a swan of the Lord. Our senses are defiled by the organs, like that of a crane.' Then Baba recited the fourth Stanza:-

*If Thou so blesseth, O Merciful Master, the crane is again transformed into the swan. Prays Nanak, the slave of Thine slave, O My Merciful Master, have Thou mercy upon me. 4.1.9 (SGGS 1171)*

The Pandit uttered: 'O Revered One! You are a devotee of the Lord. Please sanctify and enlighten this town. Bless it and in return take credit from here.' Guru Nanak asked: 'What type of credit will I receive?' Then the Pandit said: 'Sir! The credit is education. On acquiring it, prosperity is attained. Wherever one sits, the world recognizes the educated and through this, one becomes a *Mahant* (the chief priest). Then Baba recited the Sabad, in Rag Basant:-

## Basant Hindol Mehla 1.

*The city is frail and the king is a boy who loves the wicked. He reads of his two mothers and two fathers.1. O Pandit, reflect thou on this. O sire pandit, instruct thou me. What is the way, by which I can attain unto the Lord of Life? 1. Pause. The vegetation flowers, though within it is fire, and the ocean is bound as if in a bundle. The sun and the moon both abide in the same sky home. Thou hast obtained not such knowledge.2. Whosoever eats up the one mammon, he deems the Lord pervading all over. Know that the attribute of such a man is that he amasses the wealth of compassion.3. The mind lives with those who listen not to advice and admit not what they eat. Prays Nanak, the slave of the Lord's slave, such is the mind that in a moment, it is great and in another moment small.4.3.11. (SGGS 1171)*

Pandit Chatur Das entreated and said: 'O Sir! Whatever we read out to the world, we read to ourselves also. How shall we acquire the Lord's Name?' Then Guru Nanak asked: 'O Swami! What do you read? And what sort of teaching do you render to the world? What education do you give to your followers?' The Pandit replied: 'O Sir! We teach the Lord's sermons; the first lesson is worth the world.' Then Baba recited:-

## Ramkali Mehla 1.

*Dakhani Onkar. Brahma was created through the One Lord. That Brahma cherished One Lord in the mind. It is from the One Lord that mountains and ages have emanated. It is the Lord who created the Vedas. It is through the One Lord, that the world is saved. It is through the Lord, that the God-conscious beings are emancipated. Hear thou the account of the Imperishable Lord, worthy of obeisance. The eternal Lord is the essence of the three worlds.1. Hear, O Pandit, why writest thou the worldly puzzles? By Guru's grace, write thou only the Name of the Lord, the Cherisher of the world.1. Pause. (SGGS 929-930)*

Following this were recited the 54 Stanzas of *Dakhani Onkar*. Hearing these, the Pandit got up from his seated position and fell at Baba's feet. He became a follower of Baba's Name and started repeating Guru, Guru! Thereafter, Guru Nanak started to proceed further on with his journey.

# 18. Discourse with Sidhas at Nanak Mata

Baba Nanak and Mardana reached Nanak Mata while traversing through the lands. They sat under a Bohr tree which had been leafless, had turned pale and was dry for many years. They rested under it and lighted fire to get warmth. While the Baba was relaxing and meditating, the tree started to turn green once again. Meanwhile some Sidhas saw it and approached the Baba and sat near him. One of the Sidhas asked: 'O young one! Whose disciple are you? Where did you get your initiation from?' The Guru Baba recited the following Sabad in Rag Suhi:-

## Suhi Mehla 1 Ghar 7.

*What is the scale, and what are the weights? What assayer shall I call for Thee, O Lord? Who is the Guru, from whom I should receive instruction and by whom should I have Thy worth appraised?1. O my venerable Beloved, I know not Thy limit. Thou art fully contained in water, dry land, nether and upper regions. Thou Thyself art pervading everywhere.1. Pause. My soul is the scale, the consciousness the weights and the performance of Thy service is my jeweler. Within my mind I weigh the Spouse. In this way I fix my attention.2. Thou Thyself art the tongue of the balance, the weights and the balance. Thou Thyself art the Dealer.3. The blind of low caste, and the stranger soul comes but for a moment and departs in a trice. In its companionship Nanak abides. How can he, the fool, attain to Thee, O Lord?.4.2.9. (SGGS 730-731)*

Then the Sidhas asked: 'O young one! You should become a yogi and join our sect and appear as one of us.' Then Baba took up a Sabad in Rag Suhi Lalita*:-

**Suhi Mehla 1 Ghar 7.**

*Yoga is not I the patched coat, nor the Yoga is in staff, nor Yoga is in smearing the body with ashes. Yoga consists not with ear-rings, or in shaven head and Yoga not even in the blowing of horn. Abide pure amidst the worldly impurities. Thus shalt thou find the way to Yoga.1. By mere words, Yoga is obtained not. He is called a Yogi who looks upon all mortals with the same eye and deems them as equal.1. Pause. Yoga consists not in wandering to yonder tombs, or crematoriums, or sitting in trance. Yoga consists not in wandering in native and foreign lands, nor in bathing at places of pilgrimage. Abide thou pure amid the worldly impurities. Thus shalt thou find the way of Yoga.2. If man meets with the True Guru, then is his doubts dispelled and wandering mind is restrained. It rains Nectar, celestial music plays and from within his mind, man obtains gnosis. Remain thou pure amid impurities. Like this shalt thou find the way of Yoga?.3. Nanak in the midst of life be thou in death. Practise thou such a Yoga. When the horn blows without being blown, then shalt thou obtain the fearless status. When man remains detached amidst worldly attachments, then attains he the way of Yoga. 4.1.8.     (SGGS 730)*

After hearing the melodious Sabad, the Sidhas offered their salutation and obeisance to the Guru. They realized that he was a great and holy person by whose divine presence the dried up Bohr tree had turned lush green once again. Guru Nanak departed from there and went on with his journey.

# 19. At the stay of Vanjaras

Guru Nanak and Mardana reached the precincts of a 1*dera* that belonged to Vanjaras, who were bangle sellers. They came to a house belonging to the tribe's leader and sat down at its door.

Recently, a son had been born at the home and the community members were coming over to offer him congratulations and their best wishes to the family. A person came over and sprinkled colour at his house; another member showered his blessings to the new born.

Mardana was sitting and watching the spectacle taking place in front of him. He felt hungry and asked Guru Nanak: 'Blessed be you, O Lord! We have been sitting here for a while and the leader of this tribe has not inquired about our wellbeing. A son has been born in his house and he seems to have developed an ego as he does not care about the welfare of mendicants. O Lord! If you may allow, I would like to go to his house. He has been offering celebratory alms to supplicants; I may also receive something.'

The Baba felt amused and said: 'O Mardana! Not a son has been born in his house; a transitory being has arrived there; do remain silent. He shall stay for the night and go away tomorrow. Since it has come to your mind to see the Leader, you may go there. But don't offer any blessing; go and stand there in silence.' Mardana said: 'Be it all well! I shall go and see for myself.'

Mardana proceeded towards the leader's house. He reached the place and stood silent as instructed. No one came about to inquire of him. After a while, Mardana got up and returned. The Baba said: 'Mardana! Play the *rabab*!' Mardana started playing the *rabab* and set it on Rag Sri Rag. Guru Baba recited the Sabad:-

## Siri Rag Pehre Mehla 1* Ghar 1.

*In the first watch of night, O my merchant friend! By Lord's order, Thou were cast into the womb. With body reversed, Thou performed penance within and prayed to thy Master, O my merchant friend! Upside down, Thou said prayers unto the Lord with fixed attention and affection. Thou came against manner (naked) in the dark age (world) and again shall depart naked. Such cargo shall be with the mortal, as God's pen has recorded on his brow. Says Nanak, in the first watch, Soul descends into the womb by Lord's will.1. In the second watch of the night, O merchant friend! Man forgets Lord's meditation. From hand to hand he is handled about like Krishan in the house of Yashoda, O merchant friend! In arms, the mortal is tossed about and the mother says "this is my son." O my thoughtless and stupid mind1 Think of God. At the last moment, nothing shall be thine. Thou knowest not Him, who created the creation. Now gather thou wisdom within thy heart. Says Nanak, in the seond watch, the mortal grows forgetful of Lord's meditation.2. In the third watch of the night, O merchant friend! Man's thoughts are fixed with (on) woman and youth. O merchant friend! The mortal contemplates not over God's Name, through which he can be delivered of his bondage. The mortal remembers not God's Name and has become perplexed with the worldly valuables. He is imbued with wife's love and is intoxicated with his youth. Thus he wastes his life in vain. With virtue he has not traded and good actions he has not made his friends. Says Nanak, in the third watch, man's mind is attached to wealth and youth.3. In the fourth watch of the night, O my merchant friend! The reaper comes to the field. When death myrmidon seizes and despatches him, O my merchant friend! No one comes to know the mystery. The secret, when death's minister is to capture and take away the mortal has been given to none. So think of God, O Man! False is the lamentation around him. In a moment, the mortal becomes an alien. He obtains just the thing with which he has enshrined affection. Says Nanak, in the fourth watch, O mortal! The real-man has reaped the field.4.1. (SGGS 74)*

On the following day, the new born departed from this world. Everyone came to the house of their leader and started mourning, wailing and weeping at his loss. Seeing this, Mardana asked: 'Sir, what happened with the new born? They were rejoicing yesterday by spreading colours; they were laughing and dancing.' The Baba recited the Saloka:-

*Salok. The mouths from where we get congratulations and receive millions of blessings, the same mouths then bewail, and mind and body bear anguish. Some are dead and some cremated, and some are thrown in the river flow. Gone is the propitiator, O Nanak, do ever praise the True One. (Not in SGGS)*

Concluding the recital, both Baba Nanak and Mardana proceeded on with their wandering.

# 20. Kingship to the Grazer

While going on their journey, Guru Nanak and Mardana, reached a field of grams. They saw a grazer working in the field who started preparing pods of parched gram. Seeing this, a thought came to Mardana's mind 'If Baba may allow, I may take one or two saplings.'

Reading his thoughts, Baba smiled a little, went and sat at the field. Seeing the Guru there, the grazer came over and placed a few pods of parched gram before him as an offering. Guru Nanak handed it over to Mardana. An idea came to the boy's mind: 'I should bring something from my house and offer it to the Faqirs.' When he got up to leave, Baba asked him as to where he was going and the boy replied: 'Sir! I want to bring something from my house for you, maybe some food as you may be hungry.' Then Guru Nanak chanted the

*Saloka*: -  Slok] sQru qyrw lyPu inhwlI Bwau qyrw pkvwnu] nwnk isPqI iqRpiqAw bhu ry sulqwn] (Not in SGGS)

**Salok.** *Thy covering quilt is the mournful sitting and Thy love is the succor. Nanak is content to praise (Him), you sit, O Sultan. (Not in SGGS)*

Due to his generous nature and the virtue of offering a handful of grams to the Guru, the young man was bestowed Kingship of a land. Baba then left from there.

# 21. Coals for *Mohurs* and Thorn in Place of the Scaffold

While they were travelling, Mardana asked the Guru: 'Where can we sit and take rest from this scorching heat?' The Baba replied: 'All will be well. We shall rest at a village when it comes by.' After walking a *Kos* from the city, they came and sat in a village. In that hamlet resided a pious *Khatri* devotee. He was passing by and caught a glimpse of Guru Nanak. After witnessing the divine presence of the Master, he would come daily to pay his obeisance and offered his services to the Baba. Shortly, it become a routine for the Khatri to see the Guru on a daily basis. He had decided to partake food or drink only after getting a reverent view of the Guru who had a profound effect on his life.

One day a Pasla shopkeeper asked the Khatri: 'O Brother! Why do you go daily to the village? At first, you used to go under some pretext.' The Khatri replied: 'O Brother! A Sadhu has arrived there and I visit him daily to receive his blessings.' The Pasla shopkeeper requested: 'Do allow me also to receive his divine glimpse.' The Khatri replied: 'You can also come and have his blessings.' On hearing this, he accompanied the Khatri to receive the Guru's benevolent sight. While on their way, the Pasla shopkeeper adjourned at a maid servant's residence. Thereafter, they would go together daily from home and the Pasla shopkeeper would call on the maid, while the Khatri would devotionally serve the Lord Guru. One day the Pasla shopkeeper said to the Sikh: 'O Brother! I do misdeeds, while you go to serve the *Sadhu*. Today I would like to make a proposal with you and see what fate may offer both of us.' They fixed a spot and said: 'If you finish your business first, come over here and wait for me and if I am early, I shall wait for you here. We shall go together later on today.' As the Pasla shopkeeper proceeded to frolic with the maid, he realized that she was not present. He felt disheartened and went over to the spot fixed earlier. While sitting and waiting, he got worried and started turning over the soil. As he removed the earth, he saw a *mohur* (gold coin) lying buried underneath. He took out his knife and started digging deeper into the soil. He found a pitcher full of coal under the earth.

Meanwhile, the Khatri after paying his obeisance to the Guru, took his leave and left for the rendezvous point. While walking, a thorn at the door slit his foot and caused him discomfort, along with pain. He bandaged his foot with a piece of cloth and started walking with one shoe on his foot and the other held in his hand. On seeing the Khatri, the Pasla shopkeeper said: 'Brother! Put on the shoe.' The Sikh replied: 'Brother! A thorn has punctured my foot.' The Pasla shopkeeper said: 'Brother! I found a *Mohur* today while you pierced your foot. This seems bizarre and we must get the predicament clarified, because you serve the Guru and I perform a shameful act; you got hurt and I was rewarded.

Both of them came into the presence of the Guru, paid their respects and revealed the day's happenings to him. The Guru ordered: 'Do not tell others what transpired today with both of you.' Then they said: 'Kindly interpret the concealed lesson so that we can understand the meaning behind today's events.' The Baba explained to the Pasla shopkeeper: 'The pitcher that contained coal, was actually full of gold *Mohurs*. It is because of the deeds performed in your previous life that you received one Mohur today. Once you had given a Mohur to a Sadhu in charity and due to that pious act of yours, you received a *Mohur*. However, you have been performing sinful acts thereafter and the remaining *Mohurs* turned into coal. As for you, devoted Khatri, you had gallows in your destiny. However, since you came to my serve, the scaffold started diminishing gradually due to your pious deeds. The scaffold eventually became a mere thorn by virtue of service and you were pierced by it on your foot, which caused you minimal harm.' Both the Khatri and Pasla shopkeeper, understood the divine message and got up and fell at the Guru's feet. They became *Naam*-repeating devotees and started chanting the *Naam*. Then Baba recited the Sabad in Rag Maru:-

## Maru Mehla 1 Ghar 1.

*Conduct is the paper and mind the inkpot. Good and bad are the writs, recorded thereon. As the past deeds drive the man, so walks he. To Thine excellences, there is no limit, O God.1. Why rememberest thou not the Lord in thy mind, O mad man? Forgetting thy*

*God, thy virtues shall dissolve away.1. Pause. The night is a net and the day too, is a net. As many as are the moments, so many are the snares. With great relish, thou ever perkiest at the bait and art ensnared. O fool, by what virtues shalt thou escape? 2. The body is the furnace and the mind the iron therein. The five fires of passions are heating it. Sin is the charcoal placed thereon by which the mind is burnt and anxiety becomes the tongs. 3. The mind turned into dross, is again, transmuted into gold, if philosopher's stone like Guru be met. He blesses man with the ambrosial Name of the One Lord and then his body and mind become fixed. 4.3. (SGGS 990)*

## 22. Emancipation of the *Thugs*

After Guru Nanak and Mardana left the village and while on their way, they encountered a few *thugs*. When the *thugs* saw the Guru, they said: 'The divine radiance emanating from this person's face is astonishing, he can't be empty handed. He has a lot of wealth in his possession, although it is concealed from us.' The *thugs* came near and surrounded the Baba.

When they saw the divine view of the Guru, they became internally powerless. On seeing their expressions, the Guru asked: 'Who are you?' They replied: 'We are *thugs*. We have come to kill you'. The Baba said: 'All be well with you! Do one task before killing me.' They said: 'What is it you want?' The Baba said: 'The smoke that you see emanating over there, bring some fire from it. 1Bury us after killing!' The *thugs* said: 'Why are we talking about fire, kill and finish?' Then one among them said: 'We have killed many people. But no one has asked us to kill them willingly as you are requesting this without any hesitation and with a smile on your face. Where shall you escape to from us, we will bring the fire?'

Then the two *thugs* proceeded towards the place where fire was burning. As they reached the spot, they saw a pyre was burning there. To their surprise, they saw Good and Evil angels were standing and arguing with each other. The *thugs* asked them: 'Who are you? Why do you quarrel amongst yourself?' The angels replied: 'We are the Evil angels and by the permission of the Lord, we are taking this person to the lowest hell. These Good angels have just arrived and want to forcibly take him from us. You ask them as to why they are abducting him?'

The *thugs* inquired: 'Why are you forcibly taking him, from them?' They replied: 'This man was a colossal sinner, he was to be put in the lowest hell. But the Lord manifest, whom you have come to kill, his vision has caught the sight of smoke emanating from this pyre. Due to the Guru's divine and benevolent vision, this sinner has been blessed to reside in paradise.'

The *thugs,* on hearing this, came running back to their companions. They said: 'The one who has been emancipated by virtue of this Guru's mere sight, we had come to kill him.' They realized their mistake and with remorse in their hearts, fell at the Guru's feet. The other companions asked: 'What has happened; why are you touching his feet?' They narrated the entire story to others and everyone realized that they were in the presence of a holy man.' Soon after, the entire company of *thugs* observed the divine presence of the Guru and asked for his blessings. They stood with their hands folded, started beseeching and pleaded: 'O Lord! Kindly accept us as your *Name* followers. Do rescue us of our sins. We have committed grave transgressions.'

Guru Nanak became gracious, and said: 'Your sins shall be acquitted when you relinquish this cruel work. You should start farming as a profession. Whatever extra you earn, give it to charity in the Lord's Name. Offer your earnings to feed the ascetics and *bhagats*.' The entire company of *thugs* submitted to the directive and whatever material was in their possession, was brought and placed before the Guru. They started repeating Guru's Name, and began living their life by working hard and earning by means of honest livelihood.

The Baba recited the *Sabad* in Rag Sri Rag:-

## Siri Rag Mehla 1.

*Avarice is a dog, falsehood the sweeper and cheating the eating of a carrion. Slandering others solely amounts to putting other's filth in one's own mouth and fire of wrath is a parish. In such sins, sweet and saline savour, and self praise. I am engrossed. These are my doings, O my Creator! O Brother!.1. Utter the words which may bring honour. Good are they who are styled good in Lord's Court. The devilish sit and bewail.1. Pause. The pleasure of gold, pleasure of silver and damsel, pleasure of fragrance of sandal, pleasure of horses, pleasure of common cushion with a houri and a palace, pleasure of sweets and pleasure of meats, so many are the relishes of the human body. How can then God's Name secure an abode within the heart?.2. The words by speaking which honour is obtained, that utterance of the words becomes acceptable. By uttering harsh words, man comes to grief. Hearken, O my foolish ignorant soul! They, who are pleasing to Him, are good. What else is to be said or described?3. Wisdom, honour and wealth in the lap of those in whose mind God remains permeated. What praise of their's can one chime? What more decoration they need? Nanak, they who are bereft of God's glance cherish not fondness for charity and the Name. 4.4. (SGGS 15)*

## Salok Mehla 1.

*One without Divine knowledge sings sermons. The hungry Mulla turns his own home into a mosque. Becoming an idle-do-nothing, he has ears pierced. Another one, embracing mendicancy loses his caste. Fall not thou ever at the feet of him, who calls himself a Guru and a spiritual preceptor and goes begging. He who eats what he earns through his earnest labour, and from his hand gives something in charity, he alone, O Nanak, know the true way of life.1. (SGGS 1245)*

The Guru felt pleased at what he saw and continued on his journey. Say *Waheguru!*

# 23. Emancipation of Noor Shah

Guru Nanak and Mardana, during their travels reached the state of Kauru. On the way, Mardana felt hungry and requested: 'O Reverend Lord! May I be permitted, to visit the city! The Baba replied: 'O Mardana! This is the Kauru state and it is ruled by women who practice magical charms. If you like, you may go there; however, be careful'.

On obtaining the Guru's permission, Mardana paid his respects and proceeded to the city. While he was exploring, he saw a house which belonged to a woman and stood at its door-step. The owner asked him to come near and said: 'Are you seeking alms?' On receiving affirmation from Mardana, she invited him inside her house. As he went in, she tied a magical thread around his neck which made him turn into a lamb.

After tying Mardana (who had turned into a lamb), she went out to fetch water. The all-knowing Baba Nanak, through his divine vision saw what had happened to his devotee. The Baba reached the woman's house to rescue his companion. On seeing the Baba, Mardana started bleating, meanwhile the woman returned to her home with a pitcher of water. Baba Nanak asked the woman: 'Have you seen my companion come over here?' She replied un-hesitantly: 'No one has come here; have a look for yourself'. The Baba spoke:-

*Salok. Traders of barren soil ask for musk in bargain. But for the conduct of character, O Nanak, how can they meet the Spouse? (Not in SGGS)*

After the Baba recited the salok, the woman noticed that the pitcher got affixed to her head; she was unable to move it from there. In order to conceive the fact that it was permanently stuck on her head, she pretended that she was carrying water while going about the city, doing her daily chores.

Meanwhile, Noor Shah, who was the head of the city got the news that a sorcerer had come there and had performed a spell on a woman due to which a pitcher was permanently stuck to her head. Enraged, Noor Shah ordered the inhabitants: 'Any sorcerer who is in the city shall be punished if they are unable to resolve the woman's plight.'

On hearing the orders, sorcerer from every nook of the city came with their charms to address the issue. Some came riding on a tree, while others came riding on the moon. There was one who arrived while riding on a wall. There was a magician, who brought a garden with her, while another came beating a drum. After reaching at the woman's house, they started displaying their magical powers, by tying enchanted threads around her.

While this was going on, Baba Nanak turned towards Mardana, who was still in the form of a lamb and he started bleating. Baba laughed, and said: 'Mardana! Say *Waheguru*, and offer obeisance.' As soon as Mardana said these divine words, the thread round his neck broke and fell down and he turned back to himself with the *rabab* in his hand. Baba Nanak then asked him: 'Mardana! Play the *rabab*'. Mardana played the *rabab*. Baba recited the *Sabad* in Rag Vadhans Mehla 1:-

*The virtuous wife enjoys her Spouse. Why does the one without any merit bewail? If she becomes virtuous, then she too shall go to enjoy her Spouse.1. My Spouse is a treasure of ambrosia, why should a woman enjoy any other?1. Pause. If the bride does virtuous deeds and turns her heart into a thread, she then strings her Spouse's mind threon like a jewel, which cannot be obtained for any price.2. I ask from others the path but walk not the way shown to me and yet I say I have reached my destination. With thee, O my Spouse, I speak not; how can I, then, have an abode in thy house?3. Nanak, without the One Lord, there is not any other. If the bride remains attached to Thee, she too shall enjoy (Thee) her Spouse.4.2. (SGGS 557)*

Meanwhile, the sorcerers were unable to remove the pitcher from the woman's head and Noor Shah was informed that none of the charms worked in elevating the woman's distress. As Noor Shah was the leader of the warlocks, she along with her prominent disciples decided to take up the matter in her own hands and remove the curse from the woman.

She, along with her entourage proceeded to the woman's home and brought along her scriptures with her. On the way, she proceeded majestically, by displayed pomp and show and tried to impress the inhabitants of the city. On reaching the destination, they started reciting their magical charms and showcased their wizardly skills. Then Guru Nanak recited a *Sabad* in Rag Suhi M:1:-

## Rag Suhi Mehla 1 Kuchajji.

*I am ill-mannered. In me are infinite demerits. How can I go to enjoy my Spouse? Amongst my Spouse's brides, one is better than the other. Who is there, that knows my Name even? The mates who enjoy their groom, they are in the shade of mango (very fortunate). I possess not their virtues. To whom should I attribute the blame? What merits of Thine O Lord, should I narrate? Which, O which Names of Thine shall I take (utter)? I can reach not upto even one virtue of thine. I am ever a sacrifice unto Thee. Gold, silver, pearls and rubies are indeed bkiss-bestowing. Such things my Bridegroom has given to me and I have fixed my heart with them. The palaces raised by bricks and mud are adorned with stones. I am gone astray in these decorations and sit not near that Bridegroom of mine. The floricans shriek in the sky and the herons come and sit down. The bride goes to her Father-in-law's. Going hereafter, what face shall she show? She has forgotten her journey and was soundly sleeping, when the day dawned. Separating from Thee, O Spouse, she has amassed pain for herself. In Thee, O Lord, are merits and in me all demerits. This alone is is the prayer of Nanak. All the nights are for the virtuous brides. May I an unchaste one obtain a night as well.1. (SGGS 762)*

Guru Nanak was observing the entertaining display of sorcery along with the magical tricks and applauded: 'Wah! Wah!' Meanwhile, Noor Shah felt exhausted as her charms had failed to remove the woman's misery. She felt powerless and finally admitted her fault and false ego. She felt humiliated, defeated and put her face down in dismay. Somehow, the drums stood up and they started dancing and singing while this was going on. The Baba said: 'Mardana! Play the *rabab*'! Mardana played the *rabab* and set Rag Sri Rag M: 1. and Baba recited the *Sabad*:-

## Asa Mehla 1.

*The mind's impulses are like cymbals and ankle-bells and with them continually thump the drum of the world. The hermits like Narad dance under the influence of the Darkness. Where can men of continence and truth place their feet?1. Unto the Lord's Name, O Nanak, I am a sacrifice. Blind is the world and all-seeing is the Lord.1. Pause. The disciple rather feeds on his Master, and for the love of bread comes to dwell in his home. If man were to live and eat hundreds of years, that day alone would be acceptable, when he recognizes the Lord.2. Compassion is not excited by beholding the sight of the petitioner. There is no one, who receives and bribes not. The King administers justice only if his palm is greased. In the Name of God, none is moved.3. Nanak says that men are men only in shape and name. In deeds they Are dogs; this is the command of the Lord's court. By Guru's grace, if man deems himself a guest in this world, then does he acquire some honour in God's court. 4.4. (SGGS 349-350)*

Shortly after, Guru Baba recited another Saloka:-

*In words we are good, but in deeds bad. Within mind we are impure and black, but white from without. We emulate with those who stand and serve at Lord's door. They are imbued with the love of their Bridegroom and enjoy the pleasure of His dalliance. They remain powerless even when possessing power and are ever humble. Nanak, our lives become profitable if we associate with them (such brides).2. (SGGS 85)*

When Guru Baba recited this *Saloka,* Noor Shah said: 'Allure him with money.' Her attendants came with various forms of riches. Pearls, diamonds, gems, gold, silver, emerald, camphor and clothes, whatever precious items they had, they brought over and displayed them before the Baba. They started imploring: 'O Lord! Please take something.' Then Guru Nanak said: 'Mardana! Play the *rabab*!' Then Mardana played the *rabab,* and set it on Rag Tilang. *Sabad* M: 1:-

## Tilang M:1.

*O silly woman! Why takest thou pride? Why enjoyest thou not the love of God, in thy own home? The Bridegroom is quite near, O foolish bride. What for searchest thou abroad? Put the salve needles of God's fear into thine eyes and make the decorations of the Lord's love. Then alone shalt thou be known as devoted wife, attached to the spouse, if thou bearest Him love.1. What can the silly young bride do, if she pleases not her Groom? Though she may make good many implorations, yet, such a bride cannot obtain her spouse's mansion. Without good deeds, nothing can be obtained though she may run about a great deal. Inebriated with avarice, covetousness and pride, she is engrossed in worldliness. By these things, the Groom is obtained not.2. Ignorant is the young bride. Go and ask the chaste brides, by what actions is the spouse obtained. Whatever the Lord does, accept that as good and do away with thy cleverness and will. Attach thou thy mind to His feet, by whose love the wealth of emancipation is attained. Do thou that, what the spouse bids thee. Surrender thy body and soul to Him and apply thou such a perfume. Thus says the true wife, O sister. By these means the Bridegroom is obtained.3. Efface thy ownself and then shalt thou obtain the Groom. What can other cleverness avail? The day when the Spouse looks with grace is of signal account and the bride obtains nine treasures. She, who is the beloved of her Bridegroom, is the happy wife. Nanak, she is the queen of all. Like this she remains imbued with pleasure, intoxicated with glee and day and night absorbed in the Lord's love. She is spoken of as comely, beauteous and intelligent, and she alone is wise.4.2.4. (SGGS 722)*

Finally, everyone gathered around, came over and fell at the Guru's feet. They stood up with cloth scarves round their necks. They started saying: 'How shall we get redeemed? And how shall the pitcher be removed from this woman's head?' The Guru Baba said: 3'Say *Waheguru* and remove the pitcher from her head. You shall also be emancipated. Do repeat and recite Guru, Guru!' Then they came and fell at Guru's feet. They became Name Reciting followers of the Guru. Say all *Waheguru*!

# 24. Kalyuga – *the God of Iron Age*

Guru Nanak, after having delivered his divine message, left the city and moved on with his journey. While treading the path set forth by the divine, he reached Udian and rested there.

Kalyug, who was the god of Iron Age, saw the Lord and decided to test him with his machinations. He was disguised when he came near the Guru. He tried to intimidate him by initiating a mighty, cyclonic wind storm, due to which the surrounding trees started to get uprooted and crashed around the vicinity where Baba was sitting.

Mardana, on seeing such powerful, stormy winds, became alarmed, petrified and exclaimed: 'Lord Reverend! You have brought us to this wilderness; we shall perish and be bereft of a grave or even a coffin'. The Guru Baba said: 'Mardana! Don't feel disheartened'. Mardana said: 'As of today, with all my years of living in this world; I have never seen such a terrible calamity, as this one, which has frightened our soul?'

Thereafter, Kalyug displayed his might by flaring up fire all around them. There was smoke and it seemed as if they were in an inferno which would eventually consume them and turn them into ash. Then Mardana lay down with his mouth covered and said: 'Life is all but gone.'

Kalyug brought about the might of water to frighten the Guru. Rain started to pour in torrents and there was downpour. It seemed that earth would be consumed by this torrential, incessant rainfall and all would drown in a mighty ocean of endless water. However, all of this display of power, didn't cause any harm to the Baba as he was aloof from the magical effects. Then Guru said: 'Mardana! Get up and sit, calm down. Play the *rabab*.' Then Mardana got up and played the *rabab*. He set Rag Maru, and Baba recited the *Sabad*:

**Maru Mehla 5 Ghar 2.**

*In the Lord's fear are the earth, the sky and the stars. Over their head, is the powerful order of the Master. The wind, water and fire are in His fear and poor Inder too abides in the Lord's fear.1. I have heard one thing, that the Lord alone is fearfree. He alone is in peace and he alone is ever embellished, who, meeting with the Guru, hymns the Lord's praise.1. Pause. The corporeal beings and gods are in the Lord's fear and the adepts and seekers die in His dread. The eightyfour lacs of beings repeatedly die and are born. They are yoked to existences over and over again.2. The optimists, pessimists and egotists and the beings created with multifarious forms abide to the Lord's fear. Thi helpless deceitful mammon fears the Lord and greatly afraid of Him is also the Righteous Judge.3. The entire creation is engrossed in the Lord's Fear. Fear-free is only the Creator-Lord. Says Nanak, the Lord is the companion of His devotees and His devotees look beauteous in His court.4.1 (SGGS 998-999)*

Kalyug appeared in the form of a devil. His head was so high and mighty that it was touching the sky. As he came near the Guru, his intimidating form started to dwindle and he eventually turned into the form of a normal human being. He stood with his hands folded in front of the Baba.

Guru Nanak asked him: 'Brother! Who are you?' He replied: 'O Lord! Don't you know me? I am Kalyug and I have come to meet you. You are a representative of the Lord Creator.' He then offered obeisance to the Baba and said: 'O Lord! Have something from me. Come into my fold.' Then Baba said: 'What are you implying?' Then Kalyuga said: 'I have everything. Ask me, I can build mansions of pearls, have the walls inset with gems, jewels and have them daubed with sandal.' The Baba recited the following *Sabad* in Rag Sri Rag:-

**Rag Siri Rag Mehla 1 Ghar 1.**

*Shall I have palace built of rubies, set with gems and plastering with musk, saffron and saw dust of eagle and sandal wood, by which yearning ambition may arise in the mind? No, lest by seeing them, I may go astray, forget Thee, O God! And Thy Name may not enter my heart.1. Without God, my soul is scorched and burnt down. I am convinced after consulting my Guru that there is no other place (except God).1. Pause. (SGGS 14)*

Kalyuga said: 'Revered Sir! May I place before you: gems, along with inlaid jewels? May I bring Indra's lovely and amorous enchantresses for you?' Then Baba recited the second Stanza: -

*Though the floor be a mosaic of diamonds and rubies and the couch be enchased with gems and a fascinating houri with emerald bedecked face invites me to the couch with love and capturing gestures. May it not be that on beholding them I may go amiss, forget Thee and remember not Thy Name. 2. (SGGS 14)*

Kalyuga said: 'If this is not what you desire, O Lord! Then think of anything that may please you: wherever it may be, whether concealed under the earth or anywhere else, I will make it appear before you, even if it is thousands of miles away.'

Then Guru recited the third Stanza:-

*Becoming a man of occult powers, were I to work miracles and command and command and summon wealth; were I to become non-apparent and apparent at will, and thereby people may have regard for me. May it not be that on beholding them I may go amiss, forget Thee and remember not Thy Name. 3. (SGGS 14)*

Kalyuga said: 'Do you have a desire to be an Emperor and rule the entire world.' The Guru recited the fourth Stanza:-

*Were I to become an emperor, raise a huge army, set my foot on the throne and, seated on the throne, were I to issue commands and collect revenue; O Nanak! All this is liable to pass away like a puff of wind. May it not be that on beholding them I may go amiss, forget Thee and remember not Thy Name. 4.1. (SGGS 14)*

Finally, *Kalyuga* realized that he was in the company of a divine being; he circumambulated around the Guru and fell at his feet. He said: 'O Lord! How shall I get redeemed?' Guru Nanak replied: 'There shall be a pious devotee of mine amongst millions of followers. By his virtue, you shall be redeemed.' Then *Kalyuga* fell at Guru's feet and Baba sent him off. Say *Waheguru!*

## 25. Keer Nagar (Land of Ants)

The Guru and Mardana proceeded on with their journey and reached Keer Nagar. The location had a desolated and chilling presence all around, the trees appeared lifeless along with other vegetation which looked dead, like the colour ash which has tones of greenish-gray that symbolizes death.

On seeing the comatose sight, Mardana felt petrified and said: 'O Lord! Let's depart from this dreary place at the earliest. We have never seen such an unbarring, terrifying surrounding with horrifying landscape. 'Guru Baba said: 'Mardana! Alien inhabitants have their ruling here; this may be the hundred jungles! Here it seems as if a child born to an animal may be devoured instantly and the egg of a snake may be eaten up within seconds. Don't be afraid, as no one will come near you and cause you any harm.'

Mardana entreated and said: 'Sir! Has anyone ever come here before?' The Baba said: 'Mardana! One day, a king had attacked with 92 khuhni soldiers on this State and reached this area. Meanwhile an ant met the King and asked: 'O King! Don't do battle here! And if you do wish to, go according to my will.' The King was amused and replied: 'What is your will?' The ant said: 'O King! My request is that you may eat this loaf of bread from me.' The King said: 'I am the King of 92 khuhnis. Why should I eat your merge bread?' The ant said: 'O King! You may do as you please and proceed with your battle.'

The King moved on and started to engage in a battle along with his mighty army. The ant felt offended and ordered the other ants: 'go and bring poison.' Then the ants went and brought mouthfuls of poison from the underworld. Whoever they touched turned into ash.

Guru Nanak said: 'O Mardana! The mighty 92 khuhnis army was destroyed, as was ordained by God and only the King was left alive. Then the ant went to him and asked: 'O King! Listen to me. Will you accept my loaf, now?'

The King stood up, humbled and defeated. He folded his hands and said: 'I accept your food.' Then the ant ordered others: 'Go and bring nectar.' There are seven pools of nectar in the underworld and there are seven pools of poison there. The ants went to the underworld and came back with mouthfuls of nectar. Whoever they touched, he stood up. The entire army of 92 khuhni got back their lives by the grace of God.

On seeing his army regain their conscious, the King along with his soldiers proceeded to have food offered by the ant. When they received the loaf of bread, they noticed that it was cold; the grass for the horses was wet and the grain was powdered down.

The King on seeing the condition of the offering asked: 'Why is the loaf of bread cold, the grass wet and grain powdered?' The ant replied: 'O King! Another Ruler had come before you and I had asked him for food, fodder and grain. Whatever has remained, I have offered it to you, your army and horses.'

The King went further and saw piles of fresh food was lying in front of him. He realized that the ants had abundant food and were indeed powerful to feed a vast amount of people. On seeing such a sight, the King's pride and ego departed and he realized his mistake. He learnt that even the smallest being can be powerful and benevolent. The King then came back home.

Guru Nanak recited the following Saloka:-

**Salok Mehla 1.** *The tiger, hawks, kites and falcons, them the Lord causes to eat grass. Who eat grass, them He causes to eat meat. This way of life He set agoing. He exhibits mounds in rivers, and the deserts He makes into unfathomable oceans. A worm He appoints to kingship, and He reduces an army to ashes. All the sentient beings live by breathing. What can breath do then, if He wishes to sustain life? Nanak, as it pleases the True Lord, so does He give sustenance. (SGGS 144)*

Mardana, on hearing this fell at Guru's feet. Say 'Waheguru!'

# 26. Be Ever-Living!

From there, they proceeded further on their journey. Guru Nanak decided to have a brief sojourn and wanted to rest at the approaching village. As they went inside the hamlet, the inhabitants didn't allow him to enter their premise; they showed no courtesy and disrespected him.

They asked the Baba to leave their village immediately and never to come back there again. The Baba closed his eyes and was unaffected by the discourtesy tendered to him and in turn blessed the village to prosper and ordained the inhabitants may perpetually reside there. Then Guru Baba recited the *Sabad:-*

*How could I hold grace per this five-elemental physical self? If I speak, am said to be babbling amuch. If I hold reticence, am called to be short of wisdom. If I keep sitting, am said to be prompting mourning. If I make a move to go, am is said to have thrown ash at head. If I make a bow, am is said to cede in fear. I get not reconciled in any way, where shall I spend my living? Here and there, O Nanak, the Creator only holds grace. 2. (Shabad in Bhai Bano Wali Bir).*

# 27. Go and Be Ruined

After leaving the village, Guru Nanak and Mardana moved on and reached the next town and its residents welcomed them wholeheartedly, offered them hospitality and were courteous. They stayed there for a night and left the next day. The Guru foretold: 'This town shall get ruined. May the inhabitants disperse to distant lands from here.'

Bewildered at what he heard, Mardana inquired: 'O Lord! What a strange justice is seen at your doorstep? Where we were denied rest, you blessed the place to prosper and the kind people who served and welcomed us earnestly, that town has been cursed to be ruined.' The Guru Baba explained: 'Mardana! If the residents of the first town go to another location, they will taint others with their ungenerous manners. If a person from this town goes somewhere new, he will bring his good qualities of care, respect and hospitality with him and teach others to be kind, compassionate and generous.' Then Mardana said: 'As it may please, you look after the welfare of people.' Then Baba recited the *Sabad* in *Rag Malar M: 1*:-

*Amidst eating, drinking, laughing and sleeping, one forgets death. Forgetting His Lord, man has ruined himself and rendered his life accursed. He is not to stay here.1. O mortal, meditate thou on the one Lord's Name. This wise thou shalt go thy home with honour.1. Pause. What they, who serve Thee, give Thee? They rather beg of and receive from Thee and cease not to beg of Thee. Thou art the Giver for all the beings; thou art the life within those beings 2... The God-conscious beings who remember God, they receive Nectar and they alone become pure. Day and night, contemplate thou thy Lord's Name, O mortal. Through it the filthy are rendered Immaculate.3. As is the season, so is the comfort of the body and so is the body itself. Nanak, beauteous is the season, in which the Lord's Name ie meditated upon. What is any season, without the Lord's Name? 4.1.*

*(SGGS 1254)*

# 28. Asa Desh – Discourse with Seikh Farid

Baba Nanak reached Asa Des. On seeing Guru Nanak approaching him, Sheikh Farid spoke: 'God be with you, O holy man!' Guru Baba replied: 'Holy be the Lord! Farid! Be ever living, O Seikh, Lord be holy!' Both of them exchanged courtesies and sat down. Seikh Farid, on seeing the radiance on Baba's face, spoke to him and had an exhaustive discourse with him on religious matters. Sheikh Farid* started the conversation with Baba by saying:-

*One is to need a suit and one is to need the Lord. Put not the leg in two boats lest you go with the merchandise sunk.*

The Guru Baba responded:-

*Holding legs in two boats and load the merchandise in both of them. Any of the boats shall sink and the other shall cross over. Be there no water and no boats and neither sink nor any get away. Wealth of Truth is the real merchandise, O Nanak, that pervades at ease. (Not in SGGS)*

Then Seikh Farid said:-

*Farida! Being attached to the witch-mammon, the world appears a false illusion. Seeing with own eyes, says Nanak, the field goes marooned.*

Then Baba replied:-

*Since aborigin has it been, O Farida, happening love with the witch-mammon. The field, says Nana, is not marooned if the watchman be alert. (Not in SGGS)*

Seikh Farid spoke :-

*Farida! The body having failed and the mind gone torn, no strength is left there. Be up, O loved one, to go to the doctor and bring some medicine. (Not in SGGS)*

The Guru Baba replied:-

*Realise thou thy True Friend. In vain is the mere utterance of the words of mouth. See thou Him within thy mind. That Love is not far from thee (SGGS 1100).*

Seikh Farid spoke in Rag Suhi:-

*Thou couldest not make the raft at the time, when thou oughtest to have made it. When the sea is full and over-flowing, then it is difficult to cross over.1. Touch thou not the saf-flower with thy hand, its colour shall fade away, my dear.1. Pause. Firstly the bride herself is weak and over and above this, her Spouse's order is hard to bear. As the milk returns not to the teats, so the soul meets not with the same body again.2. Says Farid, O my mates, when the Spouse calls, the soul departs crest-fallen and this body becomes a heap of ashes. 3.2. (SGGS 794)*

The Guru Baba replied in Rag Suhi – Sabad - M: 1:-

*Make thou the raft of the Lord's meditation and arduous toil, wherewith thou shalt cross the flowing stream. Thy path shall be so comfortable, as if there is no ocean and no-over-flowing.1. Thy Name alone is the madder, with which my cloak is dyed. My Loved Lord, this colour is everlasting.1. Pause. The dear friends have departed. How shall they meet the Lord? If they have virtue in bag, that Lord will unite them withy Himself.2. Once united, the mortal separates not again. If, however, he be really united. He, the True Lord, puts an end to this coming and going.3. She who effaces and obliterates her ego, sews for herself a cloak to please her Groom. By Guru's instruction, she obtains the fruit of the ambrosial Gurbani of the Lord.4. Says Nanak, O my mates, my Bridegroom is very darling unto me. We are the Lord's handmaidens. He is our True Husband.5.2.4. (SGGS 729)*

Seikh Farid spoke in Rag Asa:-

*They alone, who have heart-felt love for the Lord are the true persons. They, who have one thing and another in their mouth, are accounted false.1. They, who are imbued with Lord's love, remain delighted with His sight. They, who forget God's Name, become a burden on the earth.1. Pause. They, whom the Lord attaches to his skirt, are the real beggars at His gate. Blest are the mothers who bore them, and profitable is their advent in this world.2. O my Cherisher! Thou art Illimitable, Inaccessible and Infinite. They, who recognize the True Lord, their feet, kiss I.3. I seek Thy protection, O God, and Thou art my forgiving Lord. Bless Thou Sheikh Farid with the bounty of Thine meditation, O my Lord. 4.1 (SGGS 488)*

Baba spoke the *Sabad* in Rag Suhi M:1:-

*Good-mannered. As You are, so am I unto all as You, O Lord, are my capital. Comfortable I abide within You. All is well as You within me. By Thy will, Thou bestowest throne and greatness and by Thy will beggary and dependency. By Thy will, the ocean flows over the desert and the lotus blooms in the sky. In Thy will, the man crosses the dreadful world-ocean and in Thy will, he is filled with sins and is drowned in it. In His will, He becomes the blissful Spouse of mine and I am imbued with the praise of the Treasure of virtues. In Thy will, O my Groom, Thou seemest dreadful and I am undone in coming and going. Thou, O Groom, art Unapproachable and Unweighable. Uttering, uttering of Thee, have fallen at Thine feet. What should I ask and what should I say and hear? I hunger and thirst for Thine vision. Guru's instruction, I have obtained, my Lord, and Nanak's true prayer has been granted. 2 . (SGGS 762)*

After exchanging their thoughts, both Baba and Seikh Farid decided to sojourn at the Jungle for a night. Soon after, a man of the Lord came over there and on seeing the holy men, he went back home. After a while, at around mid-night, he came back to the place where the holy men were resting and brought a bowl full of milk and immersed four *mohurs* in it. Then Seikh Farid took his own separate part and left the remaining part for the Guru.

Then Seikh Farid spoke:-

**Salok.** *The Lord's meditation in its first watch yields flowers, while the latter watches of the night, yield the fruits as well. They, who remain awake, obtain gifts from the Lord. (SGGS 1384)*

The Baba replied:-

**Salok.** *The gifts are of the Master. How can one contend with Him? Some whilst awake receive them not and others He awakens from sleep and gives.(SGGS 83)*

The Baba said: 'Seikh Farid! Put your hand in milk. What is in it?' When Farid did so, he found four *mohurs* of gold in the bowl of milk. He then left the bowl and went away.

Guru Nanak spoke in Rag Tukhari Chhant M: 1:-

## Sabad Rag Tukhari Chhant m:1.

*O mortal bride, with beauteous eyes, in the first watch of the dark night, watch thou thy property. Thy turn shall soon come. When thy turn comes, who shall awake thee? As thou sleepest, thine life's sap shall be sucked by the death's courier. The night is dark, the thieves shall break into and rob thy home. What shall become of thy honour then? O my Inaccessible and Infinite Protector, hear Thou my supplication. Nanak, the fool remembers not the Lord ever. What can he see in the dark night?1.The second watch has dawned. Awake thou, O unconscious one. Guard thy riches, O mortal. Thy farm is being eaten up. Protect thou thy crop and love thy Guru-God. While thou art awake, the thief shall rob thee not. Thou shalt not go the way of Death's courier and suffer not sorrow. Thy fear and dread of death shall flee. Through the Guru's instruction, with thy mind and mouth, remember thou the True Lord, in whose power are the lamps of the sun and the moon. Nanak, even now the fool contemplates not his Lord. How can he obtain peace in duality?2. The third watch has set in and the mortal is overtaken by sleep. Through wealth, children and wife, he writhes in pain. Riches, children, wife and the world are dear to him. He pecks at the bait and is ever entangled. If under the Guru's instruction, he meditates on the Name, then he obtains peace, and death seizes him not. Coming, going and death leave him not and without the Name, he is afflicted. Nanak, in the third watch, under the influence of the three-phased mammon, the men are engrossed in worldly love.3. The fourth watch has come and the day of death is about to dawn. They, who remain wakeful, night and day, save their home. The night is peaceful for those, who under the Guru's counsel, remain watchful and apply themselves to the Lord's Name. They, who act according to the Guru's instruction, are not born again and God Lord befriends them. Their hands shake, feet and frame totter, eyes grow dim and body becomes like dust. Nanak, without the Lord's Name abiding in the mind, the mortal remains miserable throughout the four ages.4. The knot of the body is loosed; arise thou, the written order for thee has come. Revelments and comforts are banned and death takes man captive and goads him on. When it pleases the Lord, without being seen or heard, death arrests and despatches the mortal. His turn comes to everyone. The ripe crop is ever mowed down. An account of every moment and instant is taken, and the soul has to suffer for good and bad deeds. He, the Lord has so arranged the play that through the Name the angelic persons are united with their Lord. 5.2. (SGGS1110)*

Later on Baba and Seikh Farid, after taking rest, proceeded from there. When the holy man who had offered the bowl of milk returned to the spot, he saw that the bowl was still lying there. As he lifted it, to his astonishment, he found that it was filled with gold *mohurs*. The holy man felt remorseful and with a feeling of regret said: 'They were the 2religious people! And whatever I may have wished in my mind, I would have acquired in faith. However, I had brought worldly things for them, therefore I received worldly items back.' Then he took the bowl and came back home.

Later on Guru Baba and Seikh Farid reached Asa Desh. The place was ruled by Samunder who was the King. He had died earlier and his skull was not consumed by the funerary pyre, although the followers had tried hard for it to turn to ash. Numerous fortune-tellers were consulted to find a remedy for this issue. One of the wise astrologers had recommended: 'He once had told a lie and due to this sin his soul is still suffering. People of Asa Desh have always been righteous and truthful, they are hardworking. As one sows during the day is what shall be reaped later on at night.'

On hearing this predicament, the inhabitants of Asa Desh became sorrowful and started lamenting. The astrologer also provided a remedy: 'He shall get salvation only if some sadhu's foot touches him.' The inhabitants, in order to get a sadhu's foot to touch the skull of their King, found a creative way to fulfill the prophecy. They blocked the entrance to Asa Desh and kept only one door open for people to enter the town. They thought if a *Faqir* would step in, he would have to pass through the narrow door, without seeing what is beneath him and on doing so will inadvertently step on the skull.

Soon after, Baba and Seikh Farid arrived at the town. When they approached the narrow gateway, Guru Nanak said: 'Seikh Farida! Put your feet.' Seikh Farid replied: 'How can I dare to put my foot forward before you?' The Baba stepped forward and put his foot through the narrow door and immediately the skull exploded. The deceased king received salvation; the citizens of the state rejoiced and fell at Baba's feet. The Baba then recited the *Sabad* in Rag Maru M:1.

*The union of mother and father brings the body into being. On that the Creator inscribed the writ of His will. This writ relates to the gifts, light and glory. Associated with the riches, the mortal loses the Divine understanding.1. O foolish man, why takest thou pride? Thou shalt arise and depart when the Lord so pleases.1. Pause. Abandon thou the worldly pleasures, that thou mayest obtain peace and poise. Everyone has to abandon his home. None can stay here permanently. We may eat some part and treasure up the rest, if we are to return to this world again.2. Man bedecks his body and dresses in silk. He issues many commands. Making his couch easy, he sleeps thereon. Why weeps he, when he falls into the hands of death's myrmidons?3. Domestic involvements are a whirlpool, O brother. Sin is a stone which floats not. Make thou thy soul, the boarder on the boat of the Lord's fear and thou shalt float over. Rare is the One, says Nanak, who is blest with such a boat.4.2. (SGGS 989-990)*

The inhabitants of the town, in order to show their gratitude to Baba Nanak and Seikh Farid, came with loaves of bread and food. As they offered them to Seikh Farid, he would say: 'I have already taken and have it in my scarf also.' On hearing this, the populace of Asa Desh said: 'O man of God! Are you some liar from the country where Farid lives? He has a wooden loaf and whenever someone offers him loaf of bread, he says: 'I have eaten and have it in my lap also.'

On hearing these words, Seikh Farid threw away the wooden loaf and said: 'By telling a lie once, the King had suffered immensely and what shall happen to me?' On seeing what had taken place, the Baba felt pleased with him and sent Seikh Farid away as he had understood an important message of always saying the truth. Baba followed up by saying: 'Baba Farid! Lord really lives in you. But you must follow a spiritual and holy man.' Seikh Farid said: 'Be it all well!' Seikh Farid then took leave; they both cordially embraced each other and exchanged greetings.

The Baba recited the *Sabad* in Rag Siri Rag, M: 1:-

*Come my sisters and dear comrades! Clasp me in thine embrace. Meeting together, let us tell the tales of our Omnipotent Spouse. In the True Lord are all merits, in us all demerits.1. O my Creator! All are in Thy power. I contemplate over the One Name, when thou art mine, O Lord! What more do I require then?1. Pause. (They say): with the decorations of Divine knowledge, contentment and sweet discourses.*

*If she hearkens to the Guru's instructions, it is then, that the Joyous Beloved meets.2. How many are thine omnipotence and how great Thine gifts, (O Master)? Innumerable are the creatures who utter (Thine) praises day and night.*

*Innumerable are Thine forms and colours and numberless Thine castes, high and low.3. By meeting the True Guru, truth is produced, and becoming truthful man is absorbed in the True Lord. When by the Guru's teachings, the mortal is filled with Divine fear, he obtains understanding and honour welcomes him. O Nanak! The True King Himself then blends man with His Ownself. 4.10. (SGGS 17-18)*

Baba Ji stayed for some days at Asa Desh and preached to its inhabitants the message of the Lord. The entire country started repeating Guru's Name. The Baba gave his blessings to the residents and they became Guru's followers. One of Guru's sermon centres is located there. Say *Waheguru*!

## 29. Bisiar Land, Jhanda Baadhi, Jugawali

Baba Nanak and Mardana travelled and followed the path as shown by the divine. After a while, they arrived at a country called Bisiar by name.

When they approached the town, they were not allowed by its inhabitants to enter and regretfully had to move on and tried to enter it from another quarter. Wherever they went, people were inhospitable, unkind, un-welcoming and they closed their doors at them.

Meanwhile, a person by the name Jhanda Baadhi saw how his fellow residents were being impolite to the strangers. He was a pious man who empathized with the strangers; he came out and brought them to his home. He washed their feet and drank the soiled water. After performing this righteous task, he visualized the divine form of the Guru. Later on, he became a recluse. As per the Guru's grace, he joined their company and started following them1.

Wrote Jugawali M: 1:- while sitting at the sea-side shore, with sand all around, the Guru inhaled air as his sustenance. Along with him was Jhanda Badhi of Bisiar country and he acquired the Jugawali there. Jhanda was present with the Guru's at the sea-shore town where devotional and ecstatic recitation of Jugawali was taking place 2.

## 30. Mardana's Hunger got Vanished

Baba and Mardana, after following the Lord's footsteps and the path ordained by him proceeded on with their journey. They reached a far-reaching, desolate bewilderment where no living being could be seen far and wide.

Mardana, after travelling a great distance and without rest, felt famished and exhausted. He made a polite request to Guru Nanak: 'All grace to devotion unto you. We have been *dooms* – we are the low-class menial bards; we have been wandering all around and have consumed loaf-pieces by begging the world over. It seems that we are lost in this far-flung land. We have reached a vast domain of bewilderment, with no one in sight. We can get away from this place only if God willed so. If there was a lion and if it attacked us, we would be left for dead and no one will know that we existed.'

The Baba said: 'Mardana! No one will come near you. But you should be forever alert!'
Mardana said: 'How could I be alert, O Master! I have reached this desolate waste land.' The
Baba said: 'Mardana! We are not in an isolated land. We are in a living land where Lord's
*Name* comes to our mind.' The Baba recited the following *Sabad* in Rag Asa M: 1:-

*The gods, for seeing the Lord's sight, suffered pain and hunger, and roamed round the*
*holies. The Yogis and the celibates live under discipline, while others wear ochre-coloured*
*dresses and become hermits.1. To meet Thee, O Lord, they are imbued with love. Many*
*are Thy Names and infinite Thine forms and it cannot be told how many merits Thou*
*hast.1.* **Pause.** *Leaving hearth and home, palaces, elephants, horses and native land, men*
*have gone to foreign countries in Thy search. The religious leaders, prophets, the pioneers*
*and the faithful have abandoned mammon and have become acceptable.2. Abandoning*
*relish, rest, happiness and dainties, some do off clothes and wear skins. Imbued with Thy*
*Name, the affected and woe-begone mortals have become beggars at Thy gate.3. To seek*
*Thee, some become skin-wearers, begging-bowl carriers, wooden staff bearers and deer*
*skin users. Others wear hair tufts, sacred threads and loin clothes. Thou art the Lord and*
*I am a buffoon of Thine. Prays Nanak, what can my caste be? 4.1.33. (SGGS 358)*

The Baba said: 'Mardana! Develop a *Sabad-oriented* mind. But for you, Bani does not come
to your intellect.' Then Guru Baba said: 'Mardana! Play the *rabab*'! Mardana replied: 'O
Master! My throat is dry; I am extremely hungry and exhausted. I can't play the *rabab*. The
Baba said: 'Mardana! Let's go to an inhabitable area.' He replied: 'O Master! I cannot go any
further as my body has given up. I can't speak anymore. I am hungry and feel as though I
am about to die.'

The Baba said: 'Mardana! I won't let you die before it has been ordained. Be alert and agile.'
Then Mardana said: 'O Master! How can I be alert and active? I am going to die; as there
is no hope of living.' Mardana went on: 'Don't disturb me anymore, O Master!' The Baba
said: 'Mardana! Eat the fruits of this tree. Eat to your heart's content, as many as you can
consume; however, remember, don't tie any excess in the bundle you are carrying'. Then
Mardana said: 'All grace unto you.'

Mardana started eating the delicious, watery fruit and thought: 'If it may be possible, I may
eat all of these. I don't know if I may have these again for a while! I may hide some in my

bundle to consume later on! I shall eat them when I feel hungry.' Mardana took some of the fruits and put them in his bundle.

While proceeding on their travels, Mardana felt hungry again and said: 'I shall eat a few fruits to quench my hunger.' As soon as he put a fruit in his mouth, he fell down. Then Baba said: 'What happened, Mardana'? 'O Master! You asked me to eat what I could eat there and not to tie any in the bundle. I however, wanted to eat later on and due to my greed put some in the parcel, lest I may not get these again. So as I ate the fruit, I fell down and feel weak.' Then Baba said: 'Mardana! You were wrong, as you should not have eaten the fruit afterwards as they were poisonous. They had become nectar when the *word* was recited at that place.'

To remediate Mardana's alignment, Baba put his foot on his forehead and Mardana got up and felt better. Then Mardana said: 'All grace to your worship and your divineness! We, the poor lowly bards like to eat by begging. You are a blessed, great-being who can live without eating or drinking and you refrain from entering any inhabitable place. How can I sustain myself by living with you? You better send me away.'

The Baba asked: 'Mardana! I am much pleased with you. Why do you ask for leave'? Then Mardana replied: 'All grateful to your pleasure, but kindly send me off. I may go to my home.' Then Baba said: 'Mardana! How can you live without me?' Mardana said: 'I will live only if you permanently remove my constant yearning for food. Whatever be your sustenance for survival, please bestow the same on me also. If you can bless me with the ability to live without food, like you, then I may stay with you. Please promise me that you will not mind my lapses and mortal behaviour that yearns for worldly needs. If you fulfill this request of mine, I will stay with you. If you are unable to grant this wish, please send me off.'

Guru Nanak granted his wish and ordained: 'Go then, O Mardana! You have been gratified by the world over!' On hearing these words, Mardana fell at Baba's feet. Guru Baba blessed him with numerous boons and lifted his forehead. Mardana finally acquired the realization of the inaccessible and unapproachable. From there on, Mardana unquestionably followed the Baba and stayed with him during his travels. They finally concluded their itinerary and came home.

# 31. Meeting Mother and Father

Baba Nanak and Mardana completed the first phase of their travels which lasted for twelve years and finally came back home. They arrived at the outskirts of their town and rested at a distance of one Kos from Talwandi, in a desolate place. After having a brief siesta and recuperating from their long journey, Mardana pleaded: 'If I may be ordered, shall I go home and inquire about the welfare of my household. I would like to see how members of my family are keeping up and would like to know about their health and wellbeing, I am anxious to know whether my loved ones are still alive or have passed away.'

On hearing the plea, Baba laughed a little, and said smilingly 'Mardana! If your family members are no more, how will you be able to protect others in this world, when you have been unable to protect your loved ones? But if you have a desire to meet your family and inquire about their welfare, then go and visit them. But come back immediately and do call upon my father, 1Kalu's at his house also. Don't let them know that I am here.' Then Mardana offered obeisance by touching Guru's feet and went on.

He came to Talwandi and entered his home. The entire neighbourhood gathered to get a glimpse of Mardana. Friends and family came over, offered obeisance and said: 'Mardana, who is a low caste bard is now the shadow of Nanak. He is not the same person anymore. He is an enlightened being and has travelled the entire world.' Whoever came to see him, reverently touched his feet.

Mardana, after meeting his companions, went to Kalu's courtyard and sat down. Soon after, Baba's mother saw him and was delighted at seeing her son's companion. She immediately came up to him, embraced him and shortly afterwards felt sorrowful. She had tears in her eyes on not finding her son with him. While she was crying, she said: 'Mardana! Tell me about Nanak, where is he!'

Soon after, other members came over to the courtyard where Mardana was sitting. Everyone started asking him about Guru Nanak. Mardana replied to them: 'O Brothers! When the Baba reached Sultanpur I, the bard, was with him; thereafter, I know nothing about his where-abouts.' After talking to everyone, Mardana got up to leave. However, the Baba's mother was not satisfied at Mardana's explanation and said: 'You know Nanak's whereabouts, take me to him, I will not let you leave empty handed.'

The Mother brought a few garments, some sweets with her and started following Mardana. She pleaded: 'Mardana! **2**Take me to my son, Nanak.' Mardana kept silent, thinking of what to do. The Guru's mother had ordered him to bring her to Nanak and he could not refuse her command.

They left the house and after travelling for about two *Kos*, saw Baba sitting at the spot where Mardana had left him earlier. As soon as Baba saw his Mother and Mardana coming over, he got up and proceeded towards his mother. He bowed at her feet respectfully. The Mother started wailing and kissed his head. She said: 'I'm all sacrifice unto you, my son; I'm all sacrifice unto you! I'm sacrifice unto your name. I'm grateful to have a glimpse of you. I am sacrifice unto all the places, wherever you have travelled. You have made me immensely pleased by showing your face.'

The Baba on receiving his Mother's love, became overjoyed and thankful. He felt a bit remorseful for not meeting her earlier; thereafter, he laughed and said: 'Mardana! Play the *rabab*! Mardana played the *rabab*, and Baba recited the *Sabad*:-

## Rag Vadhans Mehla 1 Ghar 1.

*Unto the opium-addict, nothing equals opium and unto the fish nothing equals water. But they, who are imbued with their Lord, to them all are pleasing.1. May I be sacrificed and cut into pieces, O Lord, for Thine Name.1. Pause. The Lord is a fruitful tree, whose Name is ambrosia. They who partake of the Name Nectar are satiated. I am a sacrifice unto them.2. Thou art not visible unto me though Thou abidest with all. How can the thirst of the thirsty like me abate, when there is a screen between the tank and me?3. Nanak is Thine dealer and Thou, O Lord, art my capital. Then alone, the doubt departs from my mind, when I praise and pray to Thee. 4.1. (SGGS 557)*

Nanak's Mother placed the clothes and sweets before him. She said: 'O my child! Eat these!' The Baba replied: 'Mother! I am content and require no food.' The Mother said: 'O child! What has caused you to lose your appetite?' Guru Baba said: 'Mardana! Play the *rabab*!' Mardana played the *rabab* and Baba recited *Sabad* in Rag Sri Rag M: 1:-

*To believe in God's Name is all sweet relish, to hear it is saltish. To utter it with the mouth is sweet savoury and to hymn God's Name, I have made my spices. Love of the unique Lord is the thirty-six sorts of flavoury Nectars. This is the way of those on whom He casts His gracious glance.1. O Brother! Ruinous is the happiness of other viands. By eating which the body is crushed and sin enters the mind.1. Pause.*

The Mother asked again: 'Take off this funny looking gown (*khilta*) and wear the new clothes I have brought over for you!' The Baba recited the second *pauri*:-

*MMMind being imbued (with Lord's love) as red, verity and charity as white dress for me. To erase blackness of sin is to wear blue clothes and to meditate (on Lord's) feet is my robe of honour. Contentment is my waist-band and Thy Name, (O Lord), is my wealth and youth.2. O Brother! The happiness of other raiments is ruinous. By wearing which the body is ground and wickedness takes possession of the soul.1. Pause.*

After some time, Baba Kalu received the news of Nanak's arrival. He rode his horse and immediately came over. On seeing him, Baba got up and fell at his father's feet and offered obeisance. Kalu looked around to get a proper glimpse of his son and sat down. He then started laminating and said: 'Nanak! You may take this horse and ride home! Guru Nanak replied: 'O Loving Father! Horses don't appeal to me.' Then Baba recited the third *pauri*:-

*To know Thy way, (O Lord), is as horse, saddle and gold crupper for me. To run after virtues is as quiver, arrow, bow, spear and sword-belt for me. To be honourably distinguished are my bands and lances and Thy favour is my caste (lineage).3. O Brother! The glee of other rides is ruinous. By which mounting the body is pained and sin enters the mind.1. Pause.*

Kalu reiterated: 'O child! You come home at once. We have built new rooms for you. You must see those as you have come back after a long time. You have your family, you must meet and reunite with them. Afterwards, if you like, you may go away.' The Baba then recited the fourth *pauri*:-

*The bliss of the Name is as houses and mansions and Thy favouring glance (O Lord) is like family for me. That is the command which pleases Thee. To say more is greatly beyond reach. Nanak, the True King, takes decision without seeking others' counsel. 4. O Brother! The pleasure of other rests is pernicious. By such sleeps the body is crushed and the evil deeds override the soul.1. Pause. 4.7. (SGGS 16-17)*

Kalu pleaded again: 'O child! Please tell us the reason as to why you are disheartened and have renounced us. Why is your mind displeased at us? Please inform me. If you like, we can arrange another marriage for you. We will make sure that you have a nice marriage ceremony. We will solemnize your new marriage extravagantly, with pomp and show.' The Baba recited the *Sabad* in Rag Suhi, *Chhant* M: 1:-

*He who made the world, watches over it, and yokes the mortals to their tasks. Thine bounties, O Lord, illumine the soul and the moon of gnosis shines in the body. By the Lord's gifts, the moon of Divine knowledge shines and the darkness of pain is removed. The marriage party of virtues looks beauteous with the Groom, who has chosen the bewitching bride after assaying. The Groom has come with the accompaniment of the melody of the five musical instruments and the marriage is performed with splendor. He who created the world, watches over it, and yokes the mortals to their tasks.1. I am a sacrifice unto my spotless friends and intimates. I have exchanged the hearts with those to whom this body is attached. Why should I forget those friends from whom I have got and to whom I have given the mind? Seeing whom I enjoy pleasure, may they ever remain clasped to my soul. Ever, ever they have all the merits and not even one demerit. I am a sacrifice unto my spotless friends and intimates.2. If the mortal has a casket of fragrant virtues, he should extract fragrance from it. If my friends possess virtues, I meet them then and share their virtues. Let us form a partnership with virtues and abandoning vices walk the Lord's way. Let us wear silks of virtues, make decoration of goodness and take possession of our arena. Wherever we go and sit, let us talk with goodness and skim and drink-in the Nectar. If the mortal has casket of fragrant virtues, he should extract fragrance from it.3. It is the Lord Himself, who acts. To whom should we complain? None else does anything. If the Lord errs, go and complain to Him. If He errs, go and complain to Him, but how can the Creator Himself err? He hears, sees and gives gifts without asking and without praying for. The Beneficent Creator of the Universe gives His gifts. Nanak, He alone is the True Lord of all. It is God, who Himself acts. To whom should we complain? None else can do anything.4.1.4. (SGGS 765-766)*

Then Baba said: 'Respected Father! Respected Mother! Lord Almighty is the Creator Himself. He is not forgetful. If He has made some sort of arrangement for me, I humbly accept it and will fulfill it.' The Mother said: 'O child! Please get up and come home; leave this useless sermon. When shall we get another chance to meet you again?' The Baba then recited the *Sabad* – Rag Maru M: 1

*They, who receive the call in the last watch of the night, meditate on their Lord's Name. For them ever ready are seen the tents, umbrellas, pavilions and carriages. They who remember Thy Name, O Lord, them Thou callest in Thy presence.1. O Father, I am ill-destined and false. Thy Name, I have obtained not. My mind is blind and is gone astray in doubt.1. Pause. I have enjoyed revelments and so my miseries have flowered. Such was the primal writ, O my mother. Now my joys are few and pains plentiful. In extreme agony I pass my life.2. They, who are separated from God, what worse separation can they suffer? They who are united with the Lord, what other union is left for them? Praise thou the Lord, who creating the world-play, is beholding it.3. Through good deeds, human birth is obtained and in this life the body enjoys worldly relishes. They whose destiny's sun has set, even obtaining the human birth, they remain separated from God. But still, O Nanak, there is hope of their union with the Lord. 4.1. (SGGS 989)*

The Baba said: 'O Father! O Mother! We have come to meet you; however, kindly grant us the permission to move on. We are as yet quite unsatisfied.' The Mother asked: 'O son! How shall I feel content and peace of mind, as you have come after so many years of travelling and are leaving us again?' The Baba said: 'Mother! Please agree to my request and grant us the permission to leave happily. You shall have gratification thereafter.'

Hearing this from Nanak, the Mother became silent as she had nothing more to say or to entice her son with.

# 32. Discourse with Seikh Biraham

Guru Nanak and Mardana left their home and moved on with their journey. After seeing the sight of the mighty Ravi Chanao, he went along the desolate route and reached Pattan region, which had an impoverished surrounding around it for about three *Kos*.

The Guru sat at an abandoned place nearby. Mardana followed his master and sat along with him. Seikh Farid was the Pir of Pattan, and Seikh Biraham was the current head of the place. At morning, one of his disciples had gone to the uninhabited location where Guru Nanak was resting to collect wood. The disciple's name was Seikh Kamaal, he was a devout person who used to collect fire wood for the Pir's sacred kitchen. He saw the Baba and Mardana sitting contently in the jungle. Soon after, Mardana played the *rabab,* and Baba started reciting the *Sabad.* He rendered the *Saloka* in Rag Asa. Seikh Kamaal heard the melodious Sabad and intrinsically had an urge to talk to the Baba:-

***Thou of Thyself art the tablet, O Lord, of Thyself the pen and Thou art also the writing thereon. Speak thou of the One Lord, O Nanak. Why should there be a second? (SGGS 1291)***

Seikh Kamaal offered his supplication and reverently asked: 'O Master! Ask this *rabab* player to please repeat this couplet.' Mardana was asked by Baba to 'repeat the *saloka.*' Mardana devotionally recited the *saloka* one more time. Kamaal was enamored by what he had heard and memorized the *Saloka* by heart. He then offered his salutations, collected his wood and left the company of the Baba.

He arrived at Pattan, put aside the wood, went to his *Pir,* paid his respects to him and said: 'Salaam *Pir*! I have met a devotee of the Lord Almighty.' The *Pir* inquired: 'Kamaal! Where did you meet him?' Kamaal said: 'Salute O Faiqr! I had gone to collect wood earlier on and there was a *rabab* player (*rababi*) and with him was a pious person whose name is Nanak. He recites his own *Salokas.*' The Pir asked: 'O child! Did you also learn any Saloka?' Then Kamaal said: 'Be long-living, O Pir! Salute to you! I too have learnt a *Salok.*' The Pir said: 'Recite it for me please! I would like to hear it?' Then Kamaal said: 'O Master! He says:

***Thou, of Thyself art the tablet, O Lord, of Thyself the pen and Thou art also the writing thereon. Speak thou of the One Lord, O Nanak. Why should there be a second?      (SGGS 1291)***

The Pir inquired: 'O child! Can to please somehow interpret this couplet, it sounds enchanting?' Then Kamaal replied: 'May you ever be hale and healthy, it is all enlightening!' Then the Pir asked: 'O child! Did you have a look at the one who recited this couplet? He is a devotee of God. Take me to his presence; he has spoken God's words.'

Seikh Biraham rode in his palanquin and proceeded to see Baba Nanak; he took Kamaal along with him. On the way, when he was about one Kos from the destination, he saw Baba, sitting there in a deep thought. Seikh Biraham went and stood near him and said: 'Complements to you, Nanak!' Guru Baba said: 'Greetings to you, O revered Pir. Always live and hearty! Do come! God has been so gracious that we have had a glimpse of you.' After exchanging greetings, both met, 1shook hands and sat down.

Thereafter, the Pir started talking: 'O Nanak! I felt amazed on hearing a single couplet of yours. I insisted my disciple that I must meet the person who composed this.' The Baba said: 'O Revered! We feel gratified that we have had the honour of meeting you.' Then the Pir said: 'Nanak! Tell me the meaning of this couplet. As you say: He is One, O Nanak! Why should there be a second?' 'Who should we serve and who do we forsake? You speak of the Almighty who is One and only. The Hindus believe in many Gods. Muslims say there is only one true Lord. Who is right here and who should we follow?'

Then Baba Nanak said: 'O dear one! One is the Lord and One only. 2Serve the One and reject the other.'

*Ever and ever, serve Him, who is contained amongst all. Why serve another second, who is born and then dies. (SGGS 509)*

When Baba recited this Saloka, the Pir raised the question:-

*Farid, tearing off into tatters my entire robe, wear I just a blanket. The wear by which my Spouse is met with, that dress alone, do I wear. (SGGS 1383)*

The Guru Baba replied:-

*Why tearest thou thy rich raiment and wearest a blanket? If thou put thy mind on the right path, then, even while seated at home, thou shalt meet with the Groom, O Nanak. (SGGS 1383)*

*The bride is at home, her Groom is abroad and ever she remembers Him and pines away. She shall have no delay in meeting her groom, if she sets her intention right. (SGGS 594)*

After Baba's reply, the Pir asked:-

*Farid, when she is young, the bride enjoys not her spouse, when she grows old, she dies. Lying in the grave, the bride cries, "I could meet Thee not, O my Spouse" (SGGS 1380)*

Then Baba gave the following reply:-

*The ill-mannered soul bride is engrossed in the body-tomb. If she has merits, then alone can she enjoy her spouse, but, O Nanak, the bride abounds in demerits. (SGGS 1088)*

Then again the Pir made a query:-

*What is that word, what that virtue and what is that jewel-like spell? What is the dress, which I may wear, by which I may captivate my Spouse? (SGGS 1384)*

Then Baba replied:-

*Humility is the word, forgiveness the virtue and sweetness of tongue, the jewel-like spell. Wear thou these three robes, O my sister, then alone thy Spouse would come under thy hold. (SGGS 1384)*

*One who serves the Spouse, the Spouse becomes her. Says Nanak, leaving aside all the she-mates, the Spouse shall be of her only. (Not in SGGS)*

After Baba replied, the Pir requested: 'Nanak! I need a sharp blade with which you can slaughter an animal and if it slides on a man's neck, it must immediately get severed. Allegorically I need that blade with which the false ego can be decimated.' Baba gave the following reply:-

*The scalpel is of truth and truth the pure steel. Its make is comparably beauteous. It is sharpened on the stone of Guru's word. It is put in the scabbard of virtue. If one is killed with that, O Sheikh, then the blood of avarice will be seen to issue forth. He, who is slaughtered thus, gets attached to the True Lord. Nanak, he merges in the Lord's vision. (SGGS 956)*

When Baba gave the mystical blade to the pertinacious Pir, he said: 'Glory to the Lord who bestows what is right and who virtuously follows him is lover of the Lord. Almighty has bestowed immense benevolence. Nanak! It is sheer impertinence to question the Lord's true devotees.' The Baba recited the next Saloka:-

*There is friendship between beauty and lust and alliance between hunger and dainty viands. A greedy man obtaining wealth becomes hand and glove with it and a sleepy man deems a tiny place as a bedstead. The wrathful man barks and is ruined. The blind one is worried in vain pursuits. To be silent, O Nanak, is good. Without the Name, all that the mouth utters is but dirt . (SGGS 1288)*

Then the Pir said again: 'Nanak! Recite one ballad of the Lord. We have a doubt that a ballad can't be without two and you say one and one only. Let me see who you consider to be a rival of the Lord?' Then Baba said: 'Mardana! Play the *rabab*'! Mardana played the *rabab* and set Rag Asa on it.

Baba recited the Saloka in Asa ki Vaar – Mehla 1.

*A hundred times a day, I am a sacrifice unto my Guru, who without making any delay, made angels out of men.1. Mehla 2. If hundred moons arise and a thousand suns appear, even with such light, there would be pitch darkness without the Guru.2. M: 1. Nanak, they who think not of the Guru, and in their heart deem themselves very clever, shall be left forlorn in the reaped field like a spurious sesame. They are left in the field, says Nanak, and they have a hundred owners. The wretches bear fruit and flower but still, within their body, they have but ashes.3. Pauri. The Lord, of Himself, created His own self and assumed He Himself the Name. Secondly He made the creation and seated thereon, He beholds it with delight. Thou Thyself are the Donor and Creator and, being pleased, Thou bestoweth and showest mercy. Thou art the Knower of all and Thou givest and takest life with a word. Abiding within, Thou beholdest Thy creation with delight.1. (SGGS 462-463)*

Nine *pauris* were composed in this context. The Pir got up, shook hands and said: 'Nanak! You have realized the true Lord. There is no difference between you and the Almighty; however, kindly be merciful, so that we may also be blessed and protected by the Lord.' Then Baba said: 'Seikh Braham! May the Lord uphold your faith.' The Pir requested: 'O Respected! Impart us a word to recite the Almighty!' The Baba said: 'Yes! You will be bestowed the sacred word. He then shared it with the Pir.'

After being satisfied, the Seikh got up and Baba saw him off. From there, Guru Nanak move ahead on his journey.


## 33. Redemption of the Beggar with Leprosy

Moving through Dipalpur, Kanganpur, Kasur and Patti, Baba Nanak along with Mardana reached the town of Goindwal, where they decided to have a brief sojourn. None of the citizens of the town allowed the Baba to stay with them at their home. Finally they reached the abode of a beggar. The Baba decided to ask the owner of the hut for shelter. They noticed that it belonged to an impoverished leper. The Baba came near his abode and requested: 'O humble fellow! Let me stay here for the night.' The poverty-stricken person humbly said: 'O Sir! Even animals run away from my sight; however, it is Lord's providence that I have had a glimpse of a man's face after a long while.' He welcomed the Baba who stayed there for the night. The impoverished host, with the dreadful decease of leprosy felt somber and started to laminate and cry at his misery. To comfort his host, the Baba recited the *Sabad* in Rag 1Dhanasari M: 1.

*My soul burns over and over again. Greatly agonized, the soul is distracted and falls prey to many sins. The body, that forgets the Guru's words, screams like a chronic patient.1. To prattle much is all in vain. Without our saying, everything is known to the Lord.1. Pause. It is He, who made our ears, eyes and nose, and who has given us tongue to talk fluently. He, who putting the man in the womb fire, has preserved him, and at whose bidding, the breath moves everywhere.2. All these worldly attachments, affections and dainties, all of them are but black stains on the soul. He, who departs bearing the stains of sins on his face, finds no place to sit in Lord's court.3. Through Thine grace, O Lord, the recitation of Thy Name is attained. By attaching wherewith, the mortal is saved. There is no other recourse. Even if, one be drowned in sins, still by meditation on the Name, one is taken care of. Nanak, the True Lord, is Beneficent to all. 4.3.5. (SGGS 661)*

Then Baba became gracious, and said: 'Mardana! Play the *rabab*.' Then Mardana played the *rabab*. Baba chanted the *Sabad* M: 1 in *Rag Gauri*:-

*O my camelish stranger soul, how shalt thou meet God, thy Mother? When I obtained the Guru, by perfect good luck, the beloved came and embraced me.1. My soul, make a determined effort and meditate on the Divine True Guru. 1.Pause. O my discreet wandering soul! Remember thou the Name of Lord God. Where an account is called for, God Himself shall release thee.2. O my wandering soul! Once thou wert very pure. The filth of ego has now come and attached to thee. The Beloved Spouse is before thee in thy home. Separating from him, thou sufferest strokes.3. My darling soul, make an effort and thoroughly seek out God within thy mind. By no device can He be found. The Guru shall show thee God in thy mind.4. My dear soul, launch an attack and, day and night, enshrine love for God. United by the Guru, when thou shall meet God, thou shall go home and obtain the palace of love.5. O my wandring soul, thou art my friend. Abandon thou hypocrisy and avarice. The hypocritical and the greedy are smitten. Death awards them punishment with its mace.6. O my wandering soul, thou art my very life. Rid thou thyself of the filth of hypocrisy and superstition. The Perfect Guru is the tank of Divine Nectar. By meeting the society of Saints, the dirt is washed off.7. O my dear soul, make an effort and listen only to the instruction of the Guru. This love of mammon is widely diffused. Ultimately, nothing goes with the mortal.8. O my wandering soul, my friend, take God's Name as thy viaticum and thus obtain honour. Thou shalt have a robe of honour of God's court, and God Himself shall embrace thee.9. O my wandering soul, he who obeys the Guru, performs Lord's service under Guru's instruction. Make supplication before the Guru, O slave Nanak, and He shall unite thee with God.10.1. (SGGS 234)*

By the grace of Baba's divine light, the poor person's leprosy vanished; his body became well and the blisters disappeared. The former leper was astonished on seeing himself healed and immediately fell at Guru's feet. He became a Name-devoted disciple of the Master and started repeating Guru's Name. Then Baba left his abode to move on with his journey.

# 34. Kirian of Pathans

Passing through Sultanpur, Vairowal and through Jalalabad, Baba reached *Kirian of Pathans*. The residents of the place called themselves 'Pathans' became disciples of Guru Nanak. They brought a *sarod*, which is a musical instrument and started playing it in their neighbourhood. They called Nanak 'the breath and soul 1Nanak'. Soon, Mardana received an order to '*play the rabab*'. Mardana played the musical instrument and set it on *Rag Tilang*. Baba recited the *Sabad*:-

*He, who has made the world, also looks after it. What more shall I say, O Brother? He who has laid out the garden, He Himself knows and Himself acts.1. Embrace thou the meditation, the meditation of the Beloved, by which peace is ever obtained.1. Pause. She, who enjoys not her spouse with love, regrets afterwards. She wrings her hands and beats her head, when the night passes away.2. No good accrues from repentance when the life ends. Then alone shall she have the chance of enjoying her Beloved, when her turn comes, again.3. The true bride obtains her Husband, she is superior to me. Those merits, I possess not. Whom should I blame?4. The mates, who have enjoyed their spouse, to them I shall go to ask. I shall touch their feet and supplicate them to show me the path.5. Nanak, if the bride obeys spouse's order, applies His fear as her sandal and performs the Incantation of merits, then obtains she her Beloved.6. She, who meets with her Lord the heart's way, ever abides with Him. That is called the real meeting. However much she may desire it, she meets Him not through mere words.7. The metal blends with the metal again and love attracts love. When by Guru's grace, man obtains true understanding, then, finds he, the Fearless Lord.8. An orchard of betel may be in the house, but the donkey knows not its worth. If one knows the nature of fragrance, then alone can one appreciate the flower.9. He alone, who quaffs the Name-Nectar, ends his doubts and wanderings. He easily remains blended with the Lord and obtains the immortal status.10.1. (SGGS 724-725)*

The Pathans were captivated after listening to the devotional Sabad which was recited in a mellifluous voice, over the mystical notes of the rabab. On becoming Baba's followers, they continuously repeated 'Nanak is our Heart and Soul.' Having blessed the inhabitants with his divine grace, Guru Baba departed from there and moved on with his journey.

# 35. Saedpur Jail

Guru Nanak along with Mardana ventured further into distant lands to spread the name of the Almighty and passed through Vatala. The Baba then arrived at Saedpur **1**Jandiali. At the town, a marriage ceremony was about to take place at the house of a Pathan. The Baba was accompanied by some *Faqirs* who were devoted, honorable and dignified in countenance. The Baba and his entourage decided to take rest near the vicinity of the house that was in the process of celebrating the marriage ceremony; however, no one came by and paid their respects to him.

The *Faqirs*, after having travelled for days were tired and hungry. On seeing that no one entertained him or his company, the Baba felt disappointed and left the place along with Mardana and the *Faqirs*. They had hoped, the Pathans on seeing holy men, would offer hospitality and would provide them a meal; however, they were treated unfavorably. The Baba became incensed, **2** and enraged. He said: 'Mardana! Play the *rabab*'! Mardana played the *rabab* and Baba recited the *Sabad* in Rag Tilang M: 1:-

*As the word of the Lord comes to me, so do I utter, O Lalo. Bringing the marriage party of sin, Babar has hastened from Kabul and demands perforce the gift of our Land, O Lalo. Modesty and righteousness both have vanished, and falsehood moves about as the leader, O Lalo. The function of the Qazis and the Brahmins is over, and the Satan now reads the marriage rites. The Muslim women read the Quran and in suffering call upon God, O Lalo. The Hindu women of high caste and others of low caste may also be put in the same account. Nanak, the eulogies of murder are sung, and the saffron of blood is sprinkled, O Lalo.1. Nanak sings the glories of the Lord in the city of corpses and mentions this affair. He who has made the mortals and attached them to pleasures, sits apart and alone, and beholds them. He, the Lord, is true, true is His decision and He issues command based on true justice. The body cloth shall be torn into pieces and shreds. Then shall Hindustan remember my word. Coming is seventy eight (vikrami), they (the Mughals) shall depart in ninety seven, and then another disciple of brave Man shall arise. Nanak utters the word of truth and proclaims truth at the right time. 2.3.5. (SGGS 722-724)*

When Guru Nanak recited this *Sabad*, a Brahmin felt remorseful, brought a basket full of raisins to the Baba and said: 'O gracious Person! The wonderful *Sabad* you just recited, please repeat it.' Then Baba said: 'O Master! This will not be possible. I will not repeat it as it is over now. You have taken the time to meet us and have offered us food, therefore you are blessed. Listen to my instructions. There is a pond about twelve *Kos* from here. You must take your family with you and immediately move from this place. If you stay here, you will get killed.' Following the advice, the Bahman took his family to the place designated by the Guru. He went and sat there in the bewilderment. The next morning, the town was attacked by the Royal King, Babar, who had invaded India. As he attacked, he battered Saedpur and devastated it. He destroyed villages in the vicinity and killed all of its inhabitants including: Hindus and Muslims. He plundered and demolished the houses. Such was the devastation that Baba's *Sabad* brought about due to impertinent behavior of the *Pathans*. The noble and worthy men thought that it was a calamity of the highest magnitude witnessed by them.

God always listens to the *Faqirs* and they in turn accept God's commands: whatever the *Faqirs* ask for, God bestows upon them. The Almighty always fulfills the prayers of his genuine, devoted and compassionate followers. These pious people always remain content and keep their demands to a minimum. They have control over the five-elemental senses, remain focused by reciting the Lord's Name and never indulge in any inappropriate conduct. They remain merciful, are kind-hearted, spiritual and uncomplicated beings.' A genuine *Faqir* will always have these aforementioned attributes. Everyone must remember that if a person, regardless of the four casts, chooses to live the life and path of a *Faqir*, irrespective of any religion, whether he is a criminal or a malicious person, he must be respected and served with from the bottom of one's heart. It is our duty to make sure that after we have attended the Faqir, he is satisfied with our service and is gratified. He must never be troubled or caused any type of harm for his action3.

Then Baba and Mardana were arrested at the town, were placed in a jail at Saedpur and were handed over to the charge of Mughal Mir Khan who ordered: 'Take away these slaves.' The Baba was commanded to carry a bundle on his head and Mardana had to take the reins of a horse and walk with him. The Baba recited the *Sabad*:-

*I am a purchased servant and slave of Thine. O Lord, and I go by the Name of lucky. In exchange for Thy Gurbani, O Lord, I have sold myself at Thy shop and whithersoever Thou hast yoked me, thither I am yoked.1. What cleverness, O Lord, can Thy servant play with Thee? I can carry out not Thy command, O my Master.1. Pause. My mother is Thy slave, my father is Thy slave, O Lord, and I am a child of Thine slaves. My slave mother dances, my slave father sings and I perform Thine devotional service, O King.2. If Thou mayest drink, then I may fetch Thee water, O Lord. If Thou mayest eat, I may go to grind Thee corn. I wave fan to Thee, shampoo Thine feet and continue to utter Thy Name.3. Salt-betrayer is Nanak, Thy slave, O Lord. If Thou pardon him, it is to Thine glory. Since the very beginning and the commencement of ages, Thou art the Merciful and Munificent Master. Without Thee, salvation can be obtained not. 4.6. (SGGS 991)*

Then Mardana implored, and said: 'Master! What sort of punishment have they incurred upon us? They have shackled our feet and we are in discomfort.' Then Baba said: 'Mardana! Play the *rabab*. On receiving the order, Mardana relied: 'Lord. I am holding the reins of a horse in my hand.' The Baba said: 'Say *Wahegur* and let go of the horses' rein from your hand.' Mardana let go of the horse, played the *rabab* and set Rag Tilang on it. Baba recited the Sabad, M:1:-

*God's sermons and tales, my friend, the Guru has related to us. A sacrifice am I unto my Guru. Unto the Guru, I am a sacrifice.1. Come, and see me. O thou the disciple of the Guru, come and meet me thou. Thou art my Guru's beloved. Pause. God's praises are pleasing to God. Them, I have obtained from the Guru. They, who obey the Guru's will, unto them, I am a sacrifice.2. They, who behold the beloved True Guru, unto them am I devoted. I am ever a sacrifice unto those, who perform the Guru's service.3. The Name, O Lord God, is the Destroyer of suffering. By the service of the Guru, the Name is received. It is through the Guru that emancipation is obtained.4. They, who contemplate the Lord's*

*Name, acceptable become those persons. Unto them, Nanak is a sacrifice and forever and aye, he is devoted.5. O God, the Lord Master, that alone is Thine praise, which is pleasing to Thee. The Guru-wards, who serve the Beloved Lord, they obtain Him as their reward.6. They, who cherish love for their Lord, their soul is ever attuned to God. Meditating and ever dwelling upon the Beloved, they live and they gather God's Name.7. The Guruwards, who serve the Beloved Lord, unto them I am a sacrifice. They themselves are saved along with their families and, through them, the whole world is delivered.8. My Beloved Guru has served the Lord. Blessed, blessed is the Guru, the True Guru. The Guru has shown me the God's way. The Guru has done me the good, yea, the supreme good.9. The Guru's disciples, who serve the Guru, they are the blessed beings. Slave Nanak is a sacrifice unto them. Unto them, he is ever, ever devoted.10. The Guruward mates and companions, they are pleasing to God Himself. In God's court, they are clothed with the robes of honour. The Lord hugs them to His bosom.11. The Guruwards, who meditate on Thy Name, O Lord, bless Thou me with their vision. I wash their feet and stirring repeatedly the wash of their feet, I drink it heartily.12. They, who eat betel-leaf and betel-nut and apply and red-paint to their lips but contemplate not ever the Lord God, them, the death's myrmidon seizes and takes away.13. They who contemplate God's Name and God and keep Him clasped to their heart, death's courier draws not near them. The Guru's disciples are beloved of the Guru.14. God's Name is a treasure, but some rare one comes to know it, through the Guru. Nanak, they who meet with the True Guru enjoy peace and pleasure.15. The True Guru is said to be the bountiful donor. In his mercy, he bestows gifts. I am ever a sacrifice unto the Guru, who has blest me with Lord's Name.16. Blest, blest is the Guru, who imparts to me the Lord's message. Seeing, yea, seeing and the body of the Great True Guru, I am ever in bloom.17. The Guru's tongue utters Divine Nectar and is adorned with God's Name. The Sikhs, who hear and obey the Guru, all their cravings depart.18. People talk of the God's way. Pray, tell me, by what means can I tread upon it? My Lord God, I can tread upon this path, by taking with me viaticum of Thee and Thy Name.19. The Guruwards, who medi-tate on the Lord, they are wealthy and very wise. I am ever a sacrifice unto the True Guru and am absorbed in the Guru's hymns.20. Thou art the Master, Thou the Lord and Thou my sovereign. If it so pleases Thee, then alone can Thy devotional service be performed, O Lord.21 Thou art an ocean of merits.21. He Himself, the Lord, is manifest in many forms and Himself He is in one form alone. Whatever pleases Him, O Nanak, that alone is the good thing.22.2. (SGGS 725-726)*

While Baba was reciting this *Sabad*, Mir Khan Mughal came near them. He was astonished to see a heavy bundle was elevated in air, above the head of Guru Nanak and a horse was following Mardana obediently, without any strap. He immediately proceeded from there, informed his ruler, Babar and said: 'O Master! There is a *Faqir* who has come to our jail. He has a heavy bundle elevated above his head, without any support. He has a low caste menial with him and behind him a horse follows unattended. He goes about playing the *rabab* and sings songs in God's praise.' Then the Royal Master said: 'With such *Faqirs* present, the town should not have been ransacked.' The Mir suggested: 'Master! Let's try to test the Faqir and see if he indeed has divine powers.'

The King and Mir Khan Mughal ordered a place to be setup at a distance with corn grinders. They gave the orders: 'Grind grains for the ruler!' The Pathans, Khatri and Hindu women were arranged to sit together and the grinders were placed in front of them. The Baba was also present there and was given the equipment to grate corn. To everyone's surprise, Baba's grinder started spinning on its own and started to abrade the corn placed in front of him. The Baba didn't use his hands and the equipment started rotating by itself. While this was going on, the Emperor came over and Guru Nanak recited the following *Sabad* :-

## Rag Asa Mehla 1 Astpadia Ghar 3.

*The heads, that are adorned with tresses, and whose partings are filled with vermillion, and those heads are shaven with scissors and the throats are choked with dust. These ladies lived in palaces, but now they are not allowed to sit even near the palaces.1. Hail! Father, hail! O Primal Lord! Thy limit is not known. Thou continuously makest and beholdest various scenes.1. Pause. When they were married, their bridegrooms seemed handsome beside them. They came seated in palanquins, which were adorned with ivory. Water was sacrificed over their heads and glittering fans were wavwd just above them.2. They were given lacs of rupees when they sat, and lacs were offered when they stood. They ate coconuts and dates and enjoyed on the couches. The ropes are put around their necks and their strings of pearls are broken.3. Both wealth and youthful beauty, which afforded them pleasure, have now become their enemies. The order was given to the soldiers, who having dishonoured them, took them away. If it pleases Him, He grants greatness and, if it pleases Him, He awards punishment.4. If the mortal meditates on the Lord beforehand, then why should he receive punishment? The rulers had lost their conscience in merry-making, sensual spectacles and revelments. When Babar's rule was proclaimed, then no (Pathan) Prince ate his food.5. Some lost their five times of prayer, and of some the time of worship is gone. Without sacred squares, how shall the Hindu women, now, bathe and apply frontal marks? They never remembered their own Ram, and now they are not allowed to utter even Khuda.6. Some return to their homes and some meeting them, inquire after the safety of their relations. In the lot of some, is so writ that they sit and bewail in pain. Whatever pleases Him that alone does happen, O Nanak! What is man? 7.11. (SGGS 417)*

The Baba became ecstatic and appeared to be in a joyful disposition. On seeing Guru Nanak's his favorable appearance, Babar asking him for a miraculous boon. Then Baba recited the *Sabad* in Rag Tilang M: 1:-

*Whom You protect, O Merciful, no one can kill him. What praise can be attributed to You, You emancipated the uncountable ones!1. Save me, O Loved One, protect me. I am slave of yours. True is my Master, who permeates all over the water and land. Pause. You protected Jai Dev and Nama, Your Loved Ones. Whoever You bestowed Your Name, them You emancipated.2. You protected Nama, Kabir, Tilochan by virtue of clinging to Your Name. You protected Ravidas Chamiar and Dhanna, who got counted among Your Bhagats.3. Nanak, lacking caste and family, makes supplication to lift him off the worldly ocean and make (him) of Your own. 4. (Not in SGGS)*

When Baba recited this *Sabad*, Emperor Babar became euphoric, reverential and immediately came close to Baba's feet and kissed them. He said: 'God's image seems to radiate from this Faqir's face.' Thereafter, the entire captives: including Hindus and Muslims started offering their obeisance to Guru Nanak. The Emperor said: 'O holy man! Do accept some offering from me.' The Baba replied: 'Nothing is of any use to us; however, do release all of the captives held by you in Saedpur jail. Also, if something has been taken away from them, please return it.'

The Emperor Babar ordered: 'Release the prisoners and give them back their belongings.' Obeying the Emperor's orders, the captives were released from Saedpur Jail and their belongings were returned; however, no one would leave the vicinity without seeing Guru

Nanak. On the third day, the Baba came back to Saedpur to meet the inhabitants once again. When he returned, he saw that the bloodshed had ceased to exist. The Baba said: 'Mardana! What happened so'? And Mardana said: 'O Master1 It all has happened as you willed.' Then Baba said: 'Play the *rabab*'. Mardana played the *rabab* and set Rag Asa on it. Baba recited the *Sabad* M:1:-

*Where are those sports, stables and horses? Where are the drums and bugles? Where are those sword-belts and chariots? Where are those scarlet uniforms? Where are those mir-rored finger-rings and beautiful faces, which are no longer seen here?1. This world is Thine and Thou art the Lord of Universe. In a moment, Thou establishest and disestablishest. Thou distributest wealth as Thou pleasest.1. Pause.Where those are houses, gates, sera-glios and mansions, and where are those beautiful caravansaries? Where is that comfort-able couch enjoying damsels, by seeing whom one would get no sleep? Where are those betel-leaves, betel-sellers and charming fairies?2. For this wealth, many are ruined, and it has disgraced many. Without misdeeds, it is not amassed, and it departs not with the dead. He, whom the Creator Himself destroys, him, He first deprives of virtue.3. When they heard of invasion of emperor Baba, then, millions of religious leaders failed to halt him. He burned houses, resting places and the princes, cut into pieces; he caused to roll in dust. No Mughal became blind and no one wrought any miracle.4. There raged a battle between the Mughals and Pathans and the sword was wielded in the battle-field. They, the Mughals, aimed and fired their guns and they, the Pathans, attacked with their elephants. They, whose letter has been torn in God's court must die, O my brethren.5. There were the women of Hindus, Muslims, Bhattis and Rajpts. The robes of some were torn from head to foot, and some had their dwellimgs in the cremation ground. How did they, whose majestic husbands came not home, pass their nights?6. The Creator, of Himself, acts and causes others to act. To whom should we complain? Weal and woe, O God, are according to Thy will. To whom should man go to wail? The Commander issues His command and is pleased. Nanak, the mortal obtains, what is destined for him.7.12. (SGGS 417-418)*

Following this, *Babarwani* came to a conclusion. Having seen through the entire affair, Guru Nanak came back home. The Baba then recited the following *Sabad* in Rag Sorath M: 1:-

## Sorath Mehla 1.

*The Formless Lord is the Restorer of what is gone. He is the Liberator from capltivity and the Destroyer of woe. I know not good deeds. I know not Lord's devotion, and I am greedy and the lover of wealth. As I go by the Name of the Lord's saint, my Master, save this honour of thine.1. O reverend Lord, of the unhonoured, Thou art the honour. The worthless ones, my World-Lord makes worthy. I am a sacrifice unto Thy Omnipotence. Pause. As a child, out of love, and disposition commits lacs of faults, and though his father instructs and reprimands him in many ways, yet ultimately he hugs him to his bosom. So pardon Thou my past misdeeds, O Lord, and put me onto Thy way for the future.2. God, the Reader of hearts, fully knows all the state of my mind, then, whom else am I to go to tell? The Lord Master is pleased not with mere utterance of words. If it pleases Him, He preserveth man's honour. O Lord, all other shelters have I seen; Thine alone remains for me.3. Becoming kind and compassionate, the Lord Master Himself, hears my supplication. He unites me in the union of the Perfect True Guru and my mind's cares are all dispelled. The Lord God has put the cure-all of His Name into my mouth and slave Nanak, now, abides in peace. 4.12.62. (SGGS 624)*

Guru Nanak had returned to Saedpur for his final visit, he saw that the Hindus and Muslims were cremating or burying their dead ones as per their respective religious rituals. In every home, people were mourning the departed by wailing and weeping; everyone was lamenting. They were in a state of despondency. After a while, Guru Baba's frame of mind transformed from being sad to gradually being ecstatic and he recited the *Sabad* in Rag Asa Kafi Ghar 2.

*As a herdsman is in the pasture for a short time, so is the mortal in the world. The men practice falsehood and build their hearth and home.1. Awake, awake, ye sleepers, and see that soul, the dealer, is departing.1. Pause. Build houses if ye hast to stay here for ever and aye. If someone were to know it, the body shall fall and the soul shall depart.2. Why criest thou 'Alas, alas'. That Lord is and shall be. Thou bewailest for him, but who will bewail for thee?3. My brethren, ye are engrossed in worldly affairs and practice falsehood. He, the dead one, hears not at all. You only proclaim unto other people.4. Only He, who has lulled him to sleep, O Nanak, shall awaken him. If man knew his 'real home', then he sleeps not.5. If the outgoing man has taken some wealth with him, then thou too amass wealth. See, understand and realize.6. Do thy dealings, gain thy object lest thou should regret afterwards. Forsake vice and practice virtue, so that thou obtain the Real Thing.7. Sow the seed of truth in the soil of faith and practice thou the tillage of such a type. Then alone thou shall be known as a trader, if thou departest after taking profit.8. If it be Lord's grace, the mortal meets the True Guru and understands his instruction. He then utters the Name, hears the Name and deals only in the Name.9. As is the profit, so is the loss. This has been the way of the world. Whatever pleases Him that is Nanak's glory.10.13. (SGGS 418)*

Mardana, one day, made a humble request to Guru Nanak. He asked: 'All of this catastrophe happened because of one human being. Why did so many lose their lives?' The Guru Baba replied: 'Mardana! Go there under the tree and sleep. When you get up, I shall answer.'

Mardana went over and slept as instructed. Earlier on a syrupy drop had fallen on Mardana's chest while he was taking his meal. While sleeping, ants came over his body and started to go near the drop. As soon as one stung him, he killed them all by slapping his chest with his hand. On seeing this, the Baba asked: 'What have you done, O Mardana'? Mardana replied: 'An ant stung me and all have died.' Baba **6**laughed a little, and said: 'Mardana! So likewise all of the inhabitants of Saedpur died because of the fault of a single person.'

Mardana fell at Baba's feet. Soon after, the residents of Saedpur became devoted followers of Guru Nanak. There was an individual named Kalal Jharu Wala in jail who wrote down this episode. He was from Khanpur, but joined the congregation and became a recluse ever since he witnessed the carnage. Then Baba **7**moved onwards from there. Say all *Waheguru*!

## 36. Discourse with Mian Mitha

While traversing through Pasrur, Guru Nanak and Mardana reached Kotla. At that town resided a person by the name Mian Mith. His abode was a little more than half a *Kos* from where they stopped for rest. They sat down in a nice green garden and offered their thanks-giving to the Almighty.

Soon after, Mian Mitha came to know that holy men had arrived near his house and he informed his followers by saying: 'Nanak is a pious *Faqir*; however, when we meet him, he shall redeem us in such a way as cream is removed from the surface of the milk.' Around that time, Baba said: 'Mardana! Listen, what Mitha has said'? Mardana said: 'Lord, he seems to have the same attributes as you and talks like you.' The Guru Baba replied: 'When Mitha meets us, we shall probe him thoroughly, the way juice is squeezed out of a lemon.'

Thereafter, Mian Mitha got up, and said: 'Let's go, friends! We shall have a glimpse of Nanak.' The followers said: 'You have already mentioned that when Nanak meets us, he shall redeem us as one takes out cream from the surface of milk.' Then Mian Mitha said: 'A voice has come from that side 'as we squeeze juice out of a lemon, we shall squeeze him when he meets us. When cream is removed from the milk, it remains unaffected; however, when you squeeze juice out of a lemon, only the residue is left.'

In a short while, Mian Mitha reached the garden where Guru Nanak was staying and had a glimpse of the divine being. He came over and offered his greetings and sat down. Mian Mitha spoke: Gost Mehla 1:

*Prime is the Lord's Name, second is that of Prophet Mohammad. O Nanak! Acceptance at His Court becomes possible if one recites Mohammadan utterance. (Not on SGGS)*

The Baba gave a response:-

*Prime is the Lord's Name and Prophet Mohammad is the watchman at the gate. O Seikh! Better you set right your conscience, and then become acceptable at the Court. (Not in SGGS)*

Then Baba said: 'Seikh Mitha! Both have no refuge at that door. Whoever abides by thy name, shall remain.' Then Seikh said: 'So Nanak! Does a lamp glow without oil?'

**Siri Rag Mehla 1 Ghar 3.** *The undeceivable (mammon) cannot be deceived by deceiving, nor can a dagger inflict wound (on it). As the Lord keeps it, so does it live. (Under its influence), the mind of this greedy man is tossed about. Without oil, how can the lamp be lighted? 1. Pause.*

The Baba replied; Salok:-

*In this body (lamp), put the oil of the practice of reciting the religious books and the wick of Lord's fear. Light this lamp with the fire of the knowledge of Truth.2. With this oil thus shall (thy) lamp burn. Make such light and then shalt thou meet the Lord.1. Pause. When the word of (His Name) softens this body-soul and service is performed, happiness is obtained. The entire world continues coming and going.3. In the world, perform Lord's service. Then (shalt thou) get a seat in Master's Court, and swing thy arm (happily), says Nanak.4.33. (SGGS 25-26)*

Seikh Mitha entreated by asking: 'O Master! Please provide the provenance of that Quran, by reading which one may acquire acceptance? Please describe the holiness that may make one fit for the door? And what is that book that remains stuck to the heart and never departs and what is that patronage that makes the vision ever gracious?'

The Baba replied: 'Mardana! Play the *rabab*'. Mardana played the *rabab* and Baba recited the *Sabad* in Rag Maru M: 1:-

**Maru Mehla 5.** *O the slave of the Boundless Lord God, renounce thou the thought of all the worldly occupations. Become thou the dust of the feet of the absolved mortals and think thyself a traveler. Like this, O saint, thou shall be approved at the Lord's door.1. Make truth thy prayer and faith thy prayer-mat. Still thou thy desire and overcome thy hope. Make thou thy body the mosque, the mind thy priest and to be genuinely pure thy Divine word.2. Make thou the practice of the Name and the religious conduct thy 'Shariat', the first stage of moral life. Make the search for God and abandonment of the world thy 'Triquat', the second stage of the moral life. O holyman, make the silencing of the mind thy 'Marft\, the third stage and meeting with God thy 'Haqiqat' the fourth one, by which thou shalt not die again.3. Instead of reading Quran and other religious books, practice thou in thy mind the restraint of the ten sense organs or women into evil ways. Bind down thou the five (demons) or (men) with faith, charity and contentment and thus shalt thou be accepted.4. Make kindness thy Mecca and the dust of the saints' feet thy fasting. Deem thou the practice of the Prophet's word as heaven. God alone is the fairy, light and fragrance and the Lord's meditation is the sublime chamber of worship.5. He alone is a Qazi, who practices truth. He alone is the pilgrim, who has been to Mecca, who purifies his mind. He, who banishes Satan, is a Maulana, and he, whose support is the Lord's praise, is the saint.6. At all times and all moments do thou remember God, the Creator in thy mind. Make thou the subjugation of thy ten organs thy rosary to remember God and make the good conduct and self-restraint thy circumcision.7. Know in the mind that everything is but short-lived. The family, home and brothers all are entanglements. The kings, rulers and nobles are perishable. God's gaze alone is the ever-stable place.8. Thy first prayer is the Lord's praise, second contentment, third humility and fourth alms-giving. The fifth* *prayer is the restraint of five desires at one place. These are thy exceedingly sublime five times of prayer.9. Make the knowledge, that God is everywhere, thy daily worship. Make the abandonment of evil deeds the water-pot in thy hand. The knowledge that there is but one God is thy making a call to prayer and to be a good child of the Lord is the sounding of a horn.10. Eat thou the food which is rightly earned. Wash away thou thy pollution in the river of the mind. He, who knows his Prophet, is the man of paradise. Azrail, death's courier, goads him not into hell.11. Make good deeds thy body and faith thy bride. Revel thou in the True Lord's love and entertainments. Make pure that is impure. Deem thou the Lord's presence thy counsel. Let the complete body be the turban on thy head.12. A Muslim is he who is kind-hearted. He ought to cleanse his inner pollution from his mind. He should not draw near the worldly pleasures and ought to be pure like the flower, silk, clarified butter and deer-skin.13. He on whom is the grace and compassion of the Merciful Master; He is the manliest man amongst men. He is the Muslim preacher, the chief of Sheikhs and the pilgrim of Mecca, and he alone is the Lord's slave on whom is the grace of Man (God).14. Power belongs to the Omnipotent Lord and kindness to the kind Master. Unfathomable are the praise and love of the Merciful Master. O Nanak, realize thou true will of the True Lord and thou shalt be released from the prison and shalt ferry across (the worldly ocean).15.3.12. (SGGS 1083-1084)*

The Seikh Mitha said: 'O Master! The way you have eulogized the One Name, how is that the One Name?' The Baba said: 'Seikh Mitha! Who has been able to gauge the value of Name?' Seikh Mitha replied: 'O Master! Be kind and inform us.'

The Baba held Seikh Mitha's arm and took him aside to a corner. The Baba said: 'Seikh Mitha! Would you like to hear the One Lord's Name?' The Baba spoke: 'Allah'! When he said this, the other arm was reduced to ash. Seikh Mitha felt awfully surprised. As he saw, nothing was left but a handful of ash. Soon a sound was heard. It was: 'Allah'! When the word resonated, he got up, unscathed. Thereafter, Seikh Mitha came over and kissed Baba's feet. The Baba 5spoke in an ecstatic tone. After having their discussion and satisfying everyone, Baba sent off Mian Mitha. Guru Nanak then proceeded from there and moved ahead on his travels. Say all, *Waheguru*!

# 37. Redemption of Duni Chand

Guru Nanak had been travelling for quite a while and thereafter reached the banks of river Ravi at Lahore. During that time, there was one Karori Duni Chand Dhupar Khatri, a resident of Lahore. On the day of Guru's arrival, *saradh* was being observed by the residents of the city. On this day, family members feed Brahmins so that the food offered to them is in turn passed on to the departed ancestors of their family.

Duni Chand was observing saradh in commemoration of his late father and when he heard that Nanak, the hermit was in the city, he decided to invite the Guru to his abode and offer him his regards.

Guru Nanak was having a sojourn when Dhuni Chand arrived there and gave details of the ritual that was going to be performed. He mentioned that various delicacies including: milk, yogurt, sweets and other edibles would be prepared and offered to the Brahmins. He respectfully invited Guru Nanak to his home to grace the occasion. Guru Baba asked him: 'Who are you commemorating on this day?' He replied: 'I am offering *saradh* in the memory of my deceased father and as per the ritual, I have invited many Brahmins to the feast.' The Baba spoke: 'Your father has passed away and for the last three days he has not had anything to eat and you say that you will feed one hundred Brahmins and thereafter the food they consume will reach your father?'

Duni Chand made a request and said: 'O Master! Where is he?' The Baba said: 'He is lying in a deserted shelter, at a distance of about five *Kos*. He has taken birth in the form of a wolf. You should go there and take some food with you and do not be afraid when you see the animal. When you reach there, he will acquire the senses of a human being. He will be able to eat your food and talk to you.'

Duni Chand went over to see his father and brought some food with him. On seeing the wolf, he paid obeisance to it. He placed the food before the animal and enquired: 'O Father! Why have you been born as a predator?' The wolf replied: 'I had come to this world and was born to search for a perfect Guru. I was a follower of a celibate monk. He had once asked me to release a *sagauti* fish that I had caught. When my final hours came to bid adieu to this world, the scent of that *sagauti* fish reached me. It had been caught and was being cooked nearby. The smell heightened my senses and I desired to consume it. Soon after I departed from this world with a primal craving to consume the fish I had saved once. It is because I wished to eat a fish during my final moments, that I have come back here as a wolf.' Then Duni Chand heard his father' plight and soon after left the place. Meanwhile the wolf had a stomach full of food and felt satisfied.

Duni Chand came back and fell at Baba's feet on giving him an opportunity to see and talk to his father. He took Guru Baba to his home. At the entrance door, there were seven ostentatious ornaments tied above the ceiling, and each ornament was worth one lakh rupees. On seeing such expensive decorations, Baba asked: 'Whose ornaments are these?' Duni Chand said; 'O Master! All of these ornaments belong to me.' Then Baba gave him one needle and said: 'Keep this with you as I trust you and give it to back to me when we meet after this life.

Duni Chand showed the needle to his wife and told her what the Guru had asked of him. Then his wife said: 'O man of God! Will this needle go with you to after life?' Duni Chand realized his misjudgment and said: 'What shall we do now?' The woman said: 'Go and give it back to the Guru.' Duni Chand brought back the needle to Guru Nanak. He came and said: 'I will not be able to take this with me to afterlife. In fact I can't bring anything along with me; please accept it back.' The Guru Baba said: 'How will you take these precious pillars of wealth, if you can't take a mere needle along with you?'

Duni Chand understood the Guru's message, got up, and offered his obeisance. He said: 'O Master! Tell me what shall accompany me to the next life.' The Guru Baba said: 'Meditate on the Lord's Name. Offer the riches to the hungry sadhus and monks and feed them. Their blessings, shall reach you.' Then Duni Chand gave away the expensive pillars worth lakhs of rupees. The Guru's command is such that whoever obeys him, shall be emancipated. Duni Chand became a devoted follower of Guru Nanak and spent his remaining life reciting the Lord's Name. Say all *Waheguru!*

The then Baba asked Mardana to play the *rabab*. Mardana played the musical instrument and Guru Nanak recited Asa ki Vaar, containing 15 steps in relation to Duni Chand.

# 38. A Brahmin's Pure Kitchen

After completing his prolonged journey, Guru Nanak came home and spent some days at Talwandi. One day, a celibate Brahmin came to see the Baba and started offering advice and pontificated him. At that time, the Baba was partaking his meal. On seeing the Brahmin, the Guru invited him: 'Please come, O Brahmin! Have food with me.' The Pandit said: 'I don't take this type of food as it is unsanctified. I shall prepare my own meal after I ritually clean my cooking area which is typically the size of a hand-length of earth. I will then prepare my stove and have it lighted with clean and purified wood. What type of kitchen do you have? As it is not like the one prescribed for us, I will not eat food prepared from such an unholy place.'

The Baba said: 'Hand over a blank kitchen to this Pandit.' The Pandit was provided an unused place for his new kitchen. He went out and started preparing it by cleansing and sanctifying the area around. He started digging up the earth around the periphery. Wherever he dug, he found bones underneath. He kept moving about for four quarters of the day, trying to find a place without any bones or any other impurities. When he felt extremely hungry, he said: 'I may go to the Baba and have food with him.' He came and fell at Baba's feet and said: 'Kindly give me your food. I am dying of hunger.' Then Guru Baba said: O Master! The time for eating a meal has passed over. However, you may go now, prepare your kitchen and cook your food. Before you dig the earth, say *Waheguru* and everything will be all right.' The Baba then recited the following *Sabad* in Rag Basant M: 1:-

*Cooking place is of gold, and of gold are the vessels. The silver lines of the square are extended afar. The water is of the Ganges and the fire from the fire wood of Carissa carandas tree. The food is of the fine rice boiled in milk.1. O my soul, these are not at all of any account, until thou are saturated not with the True Name.1. Pause. Though man may have with him eighteen Puranas written in his hand; though he may recite by heart the four Vedas and though he may bathe on the festivals, and give alms according to the caste. Though he may observe fasts and day and night perform religious ceremonies.2. Though he may be a Qazi, a Mulla or a Sheikh, though he may be a Yogi, a wandering sage or a hermit of ochre-coloured dress and though someone may be a house-holder and the performer of religious rites. But without knowing the Lord, all are bound down and driven along by the Yama.3. As many are the beings, on the head of so many are writ their tasks. According to their deeds, they shall be judged. The foolish and ignorant ones issue orders. Nanak, the True One is the owner of the treasures of praises.4.3. (SGGS 1168-1169)*

# 39. An Ascetic Child

While staying there, Guru Nanak decided to perform *kirtan* during the latter quarter of the night. He recited the Gurbani each night and asked his congregation to regularly repeat on the Lord's Name and praise his Glory.

Nearby, lived a young boy who was seven years old. He would visit the Guru and join the congregation and devotionally listen to the kirtan and religious hymns. On the commencement of *aarti* (which is a ritual worship performed by holding lighted lamps in a tray and oscillating them around), the boy would get up and leave. The Baba observed the boy's routine. He prayed devotionally, listened to the kirtan and departed early. He asked his followers one day: 'Today, catch hold of the boy.' When the child was about to leave, after paying his obeisance, the devotees came to him and asked him to stay there.

The Baba asked him: 'O Child! Why do you come here and then stealthily leave, why do you do this? You are a young child. At this age, you should eat, sleep and play around.' Then the boy said: 'O Master! One day, my mother asked me to make fire and then I started preparing one. I noticed in order to start a fire, you have to use smaller branches because they can catch fire faster. The larger ones take time to light up and can be placed on after we have the flame going.

I realized and became concerned, lest I may not live up to be an adult and may die earlier. As a child, I can better grasp the teachings of the Almighty and understand his graciousness and be liberated. We may or may not grow older and bigger, like these pieces of wood, therefore I decided that Guru must be remembered always.'

On hearing these profound and wise words from a mere child, the entire congregation was amazed and fascinated. Guru Nanak felt pleased, and the boy fell at Baba's feet. The Guru Baba recited the following *Sabad* in Sri Rag M:1* - Siri Rag Mehla 5.

## Siri Rag Mehla 5.

*Man is a guest for a trice and moment in this world to set aright his affairs. But the ignorant man understands not and is engrossed in wealth and lust. He arises and departs (from the world) repentingly and falls into the clutches of death's myrmidon.1. O blind (man), thou art sitting close to the falling shore of the river. If thou art so pre-destined, then act up to*

*Guru's mandate.1.* **Pause.** *The reaper (of the crop of life) neither sees unripe, nor half-ripe nor ripe. Having made preparation, seizing and taking their sickles, the croppers arrive. When the Land-Lord's order is issued, and then is the field-crop reaped and measured.2. The first watch of the night (life) passes in worthless affairs and during the second, the (mortal) sleeps to his fill. In the third, he prates nonsensically and in the fourth, the day of death breaks. He who gave him soul and body never enters his mind.3. I am devoted unto, and sacrifice my life to the congregation of the righteous. Through whom, understanding has entered my mind, and I have met the Omniscient Lord. Nanak sees ever with him the Wise Lord, the Knower of the hearts.4.4.74. (SGGS 43)*

Guru Nanak proceeded from there.

# 40. Karoria

Guru Nanak decided to stay at a place near the banks of the river, close to Talwandi. As he settled down, people heard of the holy man and started visiting him in immense numbers. There was commotion in the vicinity as devotees tried to get a glimpse of him. People would say: 'Some true follower of the Lord has taken birth, his name is Nanak and he is residing nearby. He has the blessings of the Almighty and has his attributes.' Vast crowds regularly gathered there and many became his disciples. Whoever visited him felt satisfied and content. Whatever the Guru proclaimed became a reality. The disciples' wishes were fulfilled. Guru Nanak recited numerous *Saloka* which the *Faqirs* sang with reverence:-

*Falsehood shall come to an end, O Nanak, and truth shall ultimately prevail. (SGGS 953)*

At Guru Nanak's abode only One Name was contemplated upon. Everyone paid tributes to him and to the Almighty Lord, who is the ultimate Truth. Devotees from far and wide would regularly come over and visit the Guru. Whoever came, including: Hindu, Muslim, Jogi, Sanyasi, Brahmchari, Tapia, Tapisar, Digambar, Baisno, Udasi, Grihst, Bairagi, Khan, Kaneen, Umrey, Umrao, Karoriey Zimindar or landlords, were personally received by him and left completely satisfied and blessed. Everyone praised the Lord and the Guru for his presence and his benediction.

Near the place where Baba started residing, there was a village. A person by the name of Karoria lived there. When he heard the growing fame of Guru Nanak, he inquired: 'Who is he'? Who has been born and everyone repeats his name? Hindus have already been influenced by him; however, he has started to snare Muslims towards his path also. What faith do the Muslims have who trust a Hindu? Come let us go and bring him over here in shackles'?

As Karoria rode the horse, on the way, it felt frightened, shook and shuddered. He rode again the next day and while proceeding, he became temporarily blind. He felt dazed, confused, helpless and sat down. His companions pleaded: 'Master! We cannot say much as we are fearful of his wrath, but Nanak is a devout Pir, a holy man. Please offer adulation to the Lord, worship and meditate upon his Name.' On hearing this, Karoria began praising Baba Nanak.

Next day Karoria rode his horse again to meet the Guru; however, he fell down from his horse as soon as he mounted it. He was hurt and could not see anything. Soon after, people from nearby said: 'O Dewan Sahib! You were riding a horse and Nanak is a great Pir. Please visit him humbly and reverently on foot, if you seek his pardon.'

Heeding to their advice, Karoria went on foot to see the holy man. As he saw Baba's abode, he stood up and started paying obeisance to him. He came near and fell at his feet. On seeing true devotion and remorse from Karoria, Baba felt blissful and merciful. Baba asked him to stay at his dwelling for three days and offered his blessings. Then Karori made an entreaty: 'Baba! With your command, may I establish a town by your name? It will be called Kartarpur and I shall build a *Dharamsal*, place of worship here?' On receiving affirmation from the Guru, the Karori took leave. All say *Waheguru*!

## 41. Bhagirath, Mansukh and Shivnabh

Guru Nanak's father, Kalu, brought all of his men with him and came to the Baba and stayed with him. The size of his congregation increased as many followers and devotees came over to live at his abode. One day, Guru Nanak took off his robes and dressed himself with a sheet to cover his body and he took another sheet of cloth to cover his head. By doing so, he acquired the form of the impeccable, formless, the one who has been anointed to redeem the world. Everyone from far and wide came to know of the pious Baba and started repeating: 'Great, Great is Nanak. He is a Divine Bhagat born in this land.'

At that time, there was a poor and orphan Khatri who had a daughter. He was penniless and was unable to get her married as he could not afford the expenses of a decent wedding ceremony for her. He came over to the Baba and prayed: 'O Master, be kind to the poor! I can afford nothing; my daughter is a beautiful, chaste maiden and you, as per God's Name, please help me. God be gracious to you!' The Baba asked him: 'Whatever you need, write it down and we will have it brought over here. We shall pay for it.' On hearing this, the Khatri became pleased and wrote down all of his requirements to get his daughter married.

Then Baba ordered his disciple: 'Bhai Bhagirath! Go to Lahore and bring all of the items that have been written and requested by this person. Make sure that you bring each and every item listed. Remember, do not stay overnight as it will be inauspicious'. Bhagirath on hearing the command, immediately got up and went for Lahore as he was anxious to complete the task and come back as ordained.

At the city, he met a prosperous trader, and said: 'I need all these items; do get them for me. The trader said: 'You will have to stay here overnight and by tomorrow everything will be brought over to you.' Bhagirath replied: 'I have to go today as I can't stay for the night.' Then the trader said: 'All items shall be available; however, the marriage bangles, *choora* may not be available until tomorrow. The work of designing and colouring the *choora* bangles has to be performed overnight. You will have to stay for the work to be complete!' Bhagirath said: 'I will not stay here till the evening.' The trader stressed: 'You must wait till evening if you want the work on the *choora* to be complete.'

Bhagirath said: 'If the work is not complete by today and I don't arrive as ordered by my master, I will get into trouble.' The trader said: 'O Brother! How can someone's Master be so strict? Meanwhile my servants complain that I am rigid and say: 'The Master gets irritated fast and deducts wages.' You are not concerned about money and are saying: 'If I don't obey his command, I shall cause inconvenience to my master and he will be displeased with me. So who is your Master? Because of whose wrath shall your life be devastated?'

Bhagirath said: 'My Master is my Guru and if I do not act as per his order, my life shall become unsatisfactory.' The trader said: 'O Brother! What sort of Guru is he; by whose saying your life shall get ruined?' Then Bhagirath said: 'My Guru is a great and pious person.' The trader said: 'O old fellow! Where are great personages or dignitaries these days?'

Bhagirath replied: 'No, no. It is not like that. My Guru is a profound being; he is a perfect soul. He is an impeccable person.'

The trader said: 'Let's go as I would like to meet him. I have one *choora* at my home which is fully dyed and I will bring it over along with the other items. If your Guru is truly a great being, I shall accept him as my Guru and will not charge for the items. If he is not as prodigious as I thought of, I shall charge him for the entire goods.'

Soon after, Bhagirath and the Trader started to go back to Kartarpur. They were proceeding towards Guru Baba when he ordained: 'Bhagirath! Wherever you go, you keep sitting there. You are taking a long time to come back and have not replied.' They heard these words while on their way to meet the Baba. The trader, along with Bhagirath on hearing what was in his mind, became enamored with the Baba and realized that he was truly enlightened, a Great Being and Omniscient. They immediately came and fell at the feet of Guru Nanak and the trader felt contented on having a glimpse of the Guru. After bowing at Baba's feet, he felt gratified. He lived with Baba for three years, and then Baba sent him off. He learnt a good deal from Baba's *Bani* and **1**wrote it down into a book. He took leave from the Baba and came back home to Lahore.

The trader then called all of the rich merchants from the city, gave them his belongings from his shop and set on a voyage by sea to a place far off where Raja Shivnabh lived. After a while, he arrived at the town and started living there. He opened a trading business and did *kirtan* (hymn) singing at night time till the wee hours of the morning. When a quarter of night remained, he would get up and take bath with cold water.

Guru Baba had given a sermon that: 'Whoever takes bath with cold water when a quarter of night is left and who shall meditate on Guru's Name, shall receive *Amrit*, the divine nectar at the Lord's door and shall merge with the Unborn, Enlightener. Where there is Guru Baba's abode, there they shall be reposed.' The Vedas also say: 'whoever takes bath when a quarter of night is left, he shall enjoy the gratuitous of one and a quarter maund of gold. He who takes bath at four watches of night shall be gratified with one and a quarter maund of water. Whoever takes bath at rise of the day shall have neither sin nor virtue.' This is what the **2**Veda says; however, Baba has ordained, 'whoever is my Sikh, must take bath early in the morning, must pour cold water over his head and then only shall he get redeemed. He must live a contented and emancipated life till his last days.'

The trader used to regularly take bath with cold water after three quarters of the night had passed. After his daily ablutions, he would meditate and after reciting the *pothi-path*, take his meals by early morning and go for his daily business. After coming back home at night, he would sing Guru's hymns. The residents of the land used to take bath after sunrise. They had their own rituals: took anointments at the tenth lunar night (*duadsi*), on Sunday (*Amavas*) the moonless night and keep fast on (*ekadsi*) eleventh day of lunar night. The inhabitants noticed that the new trader (*bania)* did not observe any of their rituals, he didn't fast, didn't worship like they did, didn't follow the rituals for amavas, Sunday or any other occasion. Other Hindus thought that he was a polluted being, living in their city and started gossiping about his impertinent behaviour.

One day word reached Raja Shivnabh that 'there is a *bania*, who calls himself Hindu, but his manners and lifestyle are totally against their customs.' The Raja got annoyed and ordered: 'Go and bring the *bania*. I shall ask him as to why he does this. He is a Hindu and does not follow the set customs and rules.' The couriers of the Raja went and brought him in the presence of the King. The *bania* (trader) bowed his head and paid obeisance before the Raja by offering him one coconut. Then the Raja asked: 'O *bania*! You are of Hindu by birth. Why don't you keep fast and practice the normal rituals?'

The trader replied: 'O worthy Master! I have already acquired everything for which you keep fasts and for which you follow these arduous rituals. After being content with what I have, why should I abstain from food and follow any dogmas?' The Raja asked: 'What is the thing that you have acquired and feel satisfied with?' He said: 'O Master! I have had a glimpse of the dignified personage and that vision has granted me deliverance.' The Raja said: 'Have you felt satiated on having the glimpse?' The *bania* said: 'I met the Lord himself, there is nothing else to talk about satiation?'

The Raja said: 'O *bania*! What sort of a dignified personage is there in this *Kalyuga* by whose glimpse one gets emancipated?' The trader said: 'Baba Nanak is that divinity, by whose sight one gets emancipation.' Then the *bania* recited the Bani of Baba Nanak and Raja Shivnabh listened to the melodious Bani. On hearing it, he felt satiated. He felt entranced in every pour of his physical being. The Raja listened to Baba's Bani and comprehended it and said: 'O *bania*! Take me along with you where Baba Nanak is. I too would like to have a glimpse of the Guru.' The *bania* said: 'O Master! If you go like this, you may or may not reach him. You must meditate upon him in your heart. He shall come and meet you here itself.'

Raja Shivnabh said: 'Tell me the place where Guru Baba Nanak lives.' The *bania* replied: 'Baba Nanak lives at Kartarpur, about fifteen *Kos* away from Lahore. It is in Punjab. The place where he lives is called Rae Bhoe Bhatti ki Talwandi, across the River Ravi. This particular place, Kartarpur was established near the river. The holy, dignified soul resides there and He is everywhere. Wherever and whenever you remember him, he will be present there and then.'

The Raja said: 'Let's go to Lahore, and have a glimpse of him.' The *Bania* replied: 'O Master! The holy person is of such nature as no one can reach him by physically going there. You must truly and reverently remember him from within your heart and soul. Guru Baba is Omniscient and will meet you here itself.'

Raja Shivnabh agreed with the *Bania* , who took his leave. While leaving, the *bania* said: 'O Raja! You are blessed one! Guru Baba Nanak shall meet you; however, you shall not be able to recognize him. Who knows in what form he may come and offer you his glimpse! He may be in the form of a Jogi, or a Brahmin, or a stick-holder, or unclothed, or a Khatri, or an ascetic, or a sanyasi, or a celibate, or a monk, or a Hindu or a Muslim; all of these are his forms. We cannot say in what form he shall appear before you. He is an Omnipotent being. You better open up your inner senses in order to see his true form.'

The *bania* then left the place and travelled by a ship. The Raja felt dismayed on not receiving a glimpse of Baba Nanak. He perpetually started thinking of the Guru: while sleeping, sitting or when he was awake. He thought of him during all eight quarters of the day; he remained engrossed in expectation of meeting the Baba. During this time, his mind was in constant urge to meet the Guru and his heart was rhythmically beating the melancholy tune of separation from the Guru.

Meanwhile the Raja worked hard and wanted to figure out how he could comprehend Guru Nanak and recognize the genuine Master. He knew that a true Guru will not be tempted by worldly pleasures. To test the genuineness of the *Faqirs* who visited him, he arranged for beautiful, well-dressed damsels and ordered them: 'If ever, from any of the four directions comes some *Faqir* ascetic, do render him absolute service and entice him. Whoever may come, serve him well, including: sanyasi, brahmchari, jogi, digambar, vaishno, Hindu or Muslim. Serve him diligently so that he may lose his faith.' He knew that only fake ascetics will fall into the temptations and Baba Nanak will not be enamoured. If someone is a genuine devotee of the Almighty, he shall not lose his faith. In Kalyug only Baba Nanak is perfect and no one else will be like him.

During the course of time, many *Faqirs* came over in the guise of Baba Nanak; however, they fell into the trap set by the Raja. He was disappointed on not getting a glimpse of Guru Nanak. He patiently prayed to him and waited for his arrival. The Raja was convinced that Guru Nanak will one day come over to his land, meet him and bless him. He devotedly mediated on the Lord's Name. Meanwhile, the *bania* reached the land of Punjab. All say *Waheguru*!

# Second *Udasi* – The Second Travelogue

## 42. Second *Udasi* towards the Deccan

**(Saedo, Seeho and Varun)**

**God is but One and is obtained by True Guru's grace.**

Guru Nanak's second travelogue was undertaken towards the southern direction, called Deccan region. For his sustenance, the Baba used to have a handful of sand. He wore wooden sandals on his feet and in his hand, he carried a mendicant's bowl. He draped himself by wrapping a rope on his head, along with his arms, legs and thighs. On his forehead, he made a mark of *Bindli*. On his journey, he was accompanied by Saedo Jatt of Ghohe caste. After travelling for a while, the Baba reached 1Dhanasari country and stayed there for some days. During the night time, after three quarters of it had passed, his followers: Saedo and Seeho would go to the river in an attempt to serve Khauja, a holy person, whom they thought was the teacher of Guru Nanak. They were under the illusion that Guru Nanak had received his enlightenment by the grace of Khuaja.

The followers thought that, 'we may also serve Khauja at his place, beside the river and receive his grace.' One night, while going over to the river, they saw a man was approaching them with a fish in his hand. On seeing the two devotees, the man asked: 'Who are you?' Saedo and Seeho replied: 'We are disciples of Guru Nanak.' The man asked: 'Where are you going?' Saedo said: 'We routinely leave after three quarters of the night has passed and have come to offer our service to Khuaja, as our Guru has received everything, his divine gift from him.' Then Saedo asked: 'O revered one, who are you and where are you going?' The man said: 'I am Khuaja, and I go to the Guru daily at this time to serve him. Today, I am going to offer him this fish.' On hearing this, Saedo and Seeho were astonished, fell at the feet of Khuaja and said: 'O revered one! We were under the false assumption that our Guru has received divine blessings from you and here you are performing his duty. You offer your services to Guru Nanak and today, you are taking this fish as an offering to him.'

Seeing the two perplexed, Khuaja Khidar said: 'O folks of the Lord! I am water, and he is the Lord, the air. I have on many occasions, originated from him and have constantly assimilated in him.' Soon after, Saedo and Seeho fell at their Guru's feet. Foreseeing their remorse and their predicament, the Guru asked: 'Why have you come at this time?' Erstwhile, you used to come at daybreak.' Saedo and Gheho related the entire story of their meeting Khuaja and how their misconception was resolved. After hearing the story, the Baba recited Salok M: 2.*

*During the eight watches of day and night, O mortal! Destroy eight things (five deadly sins and three qualities) and in the ninth place, do subdue thy body. Within the body are the nine treasures of the unique Lord's Name. The virtuous and profound persons search those treasures. Making the Guru their spiritual guide, the fortunate sing the praises of the Lord, O Nanak! In the fourth watch of the early morn, yearning arises in the mind of the men of exalted understanding. They have friendship with the streams, and in their mind and mouth is the True Name. There ambrosia is distributed and the fortunate receive Name's gift. The body is assayed like gold and takes on the colour of spiritual progress. If the jeweler casts his merciful glance, it is not, again, put in the fire. During the other seven watches, it is good to speak the truth and sit with the literates. There vice and virtue are discriminated and the capital of falsehood decreases. There the counterfeit are cast aside and the genuine are applauded. Vain is man's utterance, O Nanak! The weal and woe are near (in the power of) the Master. (SGGS 146)*

*Air is the Guru, water the Father, earth the great Mother and day and night, the two, male nurse and female nurse, in whose lap the entire world plays. The merits and demerits shall be read in the presence of the Righteous Justice. According to their respective deeds, some shall be near, some distant, from the Lord. They who have pondered over the Name, and have departed after putting in toil, Nanak, their faces shall be bright and many shall be emancipated along with them. (SGGS 146)*

The Guru Baba stayed for some days at Dhanasari country. Numerous inhabitants of the land became Name-devoted followers and started repeating Guru's Name.

# 43. Anbhi Sarewara

At that time, there used to be a hermitage which was run by a holy man by the name of Sarewara. The inhabitants of nearby locations used to revere him immensely and worshipped him. He had heard that Guru Nanak was visiting the place, therefore he decided to meet him along with his disciples. He reached the venue where the Guru was staying and along with his followers sat near the vicinity. He asked one of his disciples to inform the Guru that he wished to meet him and have a discourse with him. Guru Nanak, on hearing the request presented himself before Sarewara and offered his respects. After exchanging courtesies, *Anbhi Sarewara* asked the Baba: 'You eat food, whether it may be fresh or stale along with parched grams. You drink cold water, eat unsanctified food and call yourself a Guru. So what merit have you received, because you kill living beings daily?' Then Guru Baba recited the following *Sabad* in Rag Majh Ki Vaar, Pauri:-

*When the True Guru becomes merciful, desire is fulfilled then. When the True Guru becomes merciful, man grieves not ever. When the True Guru becomes merciful, man knows no pain then. When the True Guru becomes merciful, then man enjoys God's love. When the True Guru becomes merciful, then what fear has man of death? When the True Guru becomes merciful, then the body is ever in peace. When the True Guru becomes merciful, then the nine treasures are obtained. When the True Guru becomes merciful, then is the man absorbed in the True Lord.25. (SGGS 149)*

*Salok M: 1.They have their heads plucked, drink dirty water and repeatedly beg and eat other's leavings. They spread out ordure with their mouths, suck its ordure and dreads to look at water. With hands smeared with ashes, they have their heads lucked like sheep. The daily routine of their mothers and fathers they give up, and their kith and kin bewail loudly. For them none gives barley rolls and food on leaves, nor performs last rites, nor lights earthen lamp. After death, where shall they be cast? The sixty-eight places of pilgrimage grant them no refuge, and pundits eat not their food. They ever remain filthy day and night, and bear not sacrificial marks on their brow. They ever sit in groups, as if in mourning, and go not into the True Court. With begging bowls slung round their loins, they walk in single file. They are neither disciples of Gorakh, nor adorers of Shiva, nor Muslim judges and Muslim preachers. Ruined by God, they walk about disgraced, and their entire multitude goes contaminated. The beings, that Lord alone kills and restores to life. None else can protect them. They go without giving alms and performing ablutions. The dust alights on their plucked heads. From within water came out the jewel, when the mountain of gold was made the churning staff. The gods appointed the sixty-eight places of pilgrimage, where festivals are celebrated and hymns are recited. After ablution the Muslims say prayers, after wash the Hindus perform worship, and the wise ever bathe. The dead and the living are purified when water is poured on their heads. Nanak, the head-plucked are devils. This word of advice pleases them not. When it rains, there is happiness. The key to the life of beings is contained in water. When it rains, there is corn, sugar cane, and cotton which affords covering to all. When it rains, the cows ever graze grass and the women churn the curd of their milk. By putting that clarified butter, havan, sacred feasts and worship are ever performed and other ceremonies are adorned. The Guru is the ocean, and all his teachings are the river, by bathing wherein greatness is obtained. Nanak, if the plucked heads bathe not, then seven handfuls of ashes be on their heads. M: 2. What can cold do to fire and how can night affect the sun? What effect can darkness have on the moon? What effect has caste on air and water? What should the earth do with chattels where-in all the things are produced? Nanak, then alone the mortal is deemed honourable, when that Lord preserves his honour. (SGGS 149-150)*

After Guru Baba recited this Saloka, *Anbhi Sarewara* became astound and understood the true meaning of the revelation. He immediately fell at Baba's feet. He became Name-devotee follower and started repeating Guru's Name. The Guru, in his ecstatic mood, concluded this Vaar of Majh in Dhanasari country. It had been written down by Saedo Ghoha.

Soon, the residents of Dhanasari country became Name-devotee devotees of Guru Nanak. A Sikh diocese is located there also. Everyone say *Waheguru!* Then Baba Ji started proceed on his journey from there.

# 44. Kauda Rakhsh

Guru Nanak, along with his companions travelled further and came near a sandy sea-shore. The place was deserted and the weather was extremely hot. At that place, there lived a demon, a ferocious monster of Dhanasari country who used to consume human beings. Guru Nanak, along with Saedo and Seeho Jats of Gheho caste reached the vicinity that was inhabited by this ravenous monster. On seeing humans nearby, the demon stealthily approached them and caught hold of the Guru.

He made preparations to consume him and started to warm up water in a large cauldron. He placed the Guru inside the water filled container that was being heated by fire. The demon was pleased on catching the Baba and felt that he would have a feast tonight. On seeing Baba's helpless condition, Saedo and Seeho panicked and started wailing. They said: 'Our souls shall also be brewed in the cauldron.' Guru Nanak, calmly and without hesitation or resistance went and sat in the hot container. He then started meditating and in an ecstatic countenance recited the *Sabad* in Rag Maru M: 1:-*

*The egg of superstition has burst and my mind is illumined. The Guru has broken the fetters of my feet and has freed me, the captive.1. My coming and going are now ended. The heated cauldron has cooled down and the Guru has blessed me with the cooling Name.1. Pause. Since I met with the saints' society, they, who spied me, have left. He, who had bound me, has released me. Then what can the death's courier do unto me now?2. The load of my deeds is gone and I have become detached from the deeds. From within, the sea, I have reached the shore. The Guru has done me this favour.3. True is my place, true my seat and truth I have made the aim of my life. Truth is the capital and truth the merchandise, which Nanak has put into his house. 4.5.14. (SGGS 1002)*

Meanwhile, the demon was getting impatient due to his lingering hunger. He saw that the cauldron was not heating up and he frantically tried to add more wood to the fire below so that it could boil the water and prepare his food faster. The water inside the cauldron meanwhile did not heat up and remained cold. The demon realized that the person inside it was no ordinary being and became petrified. To show his repentance, he fell at Baba's feet and pleaded: 'Do kindly emancipate me.' On seeing remorse emanating from the demon, the Guru asked Seeho to offer a consecrated drink to him. He became Name-devoted follower of Guru Nanak. He sought emancipation and duly received it from the divine Guru himself. Say all *Waheguru*!

## 45. Makhdum Bahavadi

Guru Nanak continued his journey along the sandy sea-shore and ahead, he saw Makhdum Bahawadi. This pious person was offering prayers, while seated on his prayer mat near the sea. Guru Baba approached him, offered his greetings and said: 'Salute to you, O holy man!' The man replied, 'Salutations to you', I am Makhdum Bahavadi Qureshi.' They both greeted each other respectfully and sat down. Then Makhdum Bahavadi asked: 'O Nanak, holy man! Let's go for a walk near the sea.' The Baba asked: 'Did you ever see something while walking about?' The Makhdum Bahavadi said: 'It happened one day, O Nanak! I had a vision of a *minar*.' The Baba said: 'Go and enquire about it.' Makhdum Bahavadi replied: 'As it be your order, Sir.'

Makhdum Bahavadi put the prayer mat in the sea and while praying, reached there. He envisioned a *minar* and Makhdum Bahavadi went close to it. As he came near, he saw twenty men were also sitting nearby. He went over and offered his greetings, exchanged courtesies and sat down. Then night fell, and twenty pots of food came down from the sky. Seeing the offerings, the *Faqirs* ate the food and kept meditating on God throughout the four quarters of the night. At dawn, the twenty men disappeared and Makhdum Bahavadi remained there that day. After a quarter of the day passed, a ship came up the horizon and started sinking before his eyes. In order to save the ship, Makhdum Bahavadi raised his hands in supplication unto God and asked 'the ship may not sink while I'm standing.' The prayers were answered and the ship was saved from sinking. When night fell, the men from previous night again came over to visit him. However, no food was delivered from the sky. Meanwhile, the *Faqirs* discussed about the Almighty, the all-powerful God and his Greatness. At dawn, the men again went away. Makhdum Bahavadi remained there on the next day also. On the second day, the *minar* started to crumble and was in the verge of getting decimated. Seeing the minar about to collapse, Makhdum Bahavadi immediately folded his hands and requested: 'May the *minar* not fall while I'm sitting here.' Miraculously, the *minar* was saved from destruction by God's grace. When night came, the men appeared again and sat together as before. This time around also, the food didn't arrive from the sky.

The faquirs said: 'Which one of you unfortunate beings has interfered in God's doing?' Then all of them started inquiring about and asked each other. Makhdum Bahavadi said 'I have saved the ship and the m*inar*.' Then the men said: 'O sane fellow! What is your name?' He replied: 'My name is Makhdum Bahavadi Pir.' The men said: 'O holy man! This is no place for Pirs or Lords as they are better suited for the living world. The door to God's abode is achieved by humility. The Pirs and Lords are not modest and hold their heads high with arrogance.'

On hearing the sermon, Makhdum Bahavadi offered his greetings and rolled up his prayer mat and put it in the sea. He tried to travel on the *musla* (the prayer mat), but it didn't move. For four quarters of the day, he kept sitting in the sea, without moving an inch. As the day passed on, the men who had appeared earlier, also came over and saw him sitting in the sea. Then the men asked: 'O holy man! Why are you sitting here?' Makhdum Bahavadi replied: 'My *musla* (the prayer mat) – does not move from here. The holy men said: 'Write Name of Satguru Nanak so that your *musla* may move.' Then he wrote 'Satguru Nanak' and the prayer mat of Makhdum Bahavadi started to move. He came to Baba, offered greetings and sat down. The Baba asked 'what did you see, Makhdum Bahavadi?' Then Makhdum Bahavadi said: 'You know everything that transpired. By virtue of your followers, I have come back and reached you.' Then Baba recited the Saloka:-

***Forsaking the Lord's praise and eulogy, the swan is attached to the skeleton, wherefore he receives hundreds of reproaches in a day and thousands in a night.1. (SGGS 790)***

The Baba ordained: 'Makhdum Bahavadi! Let go of your attachment, ego and arrogance. Recite the Lord's name and do not indulge in useless ritualistic activities.' Makhdum Bahavadi came over and kissed Baba's feet. In that context, Baba recited *Sabad* in Rag Sri Rag M:1. Ghar 2.

*Making it a halting place, the mortal sits at home, but he ever has the lurking sense to depart. If the mortals were to remain ever stable, then alone, it could be deemed to be a permanent place of rest.1. What kind of halting station is this world? Tie up viaticum of doing deeds of faith and remain attached to the Lord's Name.1.* **Pause.** *The Yogi squats in devotional posture and the Mullah sits at a place of rest. The Brahmans recite books and the men of miracles sit in God's temples.2. The demigods, perfect persons, worshippers of Shiva, heavenly musicians, silent sages, saints, religious instructors, spiritual guides and commanders have all left, stage by stage, and others too are under orders of departure.3. The kings, chiefs, angels and nobles have marched away in succession. The mortal must march away in a moment or two. O my heart! Understand that thou, too, art about to reach there.4. In Divine hymns, it is so described. Only the rare understand this. Nanak makes a supplication that Lord is contained in water, dry land, nether-region and firmament.5. He is the unseen, inscrutable, inaccessible, omnipotent and bounteous Creator. The entire world is subject to coming and going. The Merciful Lord alone is permanent.6. Call him permanent, whose head bears not a writ of destiny. The sky and the earth shall pass away. Ever-stable is He alone.7. The day and the sun shall depart, the night and the moon shall vanish, and hundreds of thousands of stars shall disappear. He alone is eternal. Nanak tells the truth.8.17. (SGGS 64)*

Makhdum Bahavadi threw away his *musla* (the prayer mat) from his hand and received the order: 'You better go and adopt some *Faqir*.' Makhdum Bahavadi asked: 'Whom should I adopt as *Pir*?' Then Baba said: 'Whom Seikh Farid has adopted.' Then Makhdum Bahavadi offered his greetings, they exchanged courtesies and Baba saw him off. Say all *Waheguru*!

## 46. Discourse with *Sidhas*

Guru Nanak proceeded on with his journey and reached up to the middle of the sea. Ahead were sitting Machhinder and Gorakh Nath, who were holy men. Machhinder saw the Guru from a distance and said: 'Gorakh Nath! Who is coming from the sea?' Gorakh Nath said: 'O Sir, he is Nanak.' Soon after, Baba appeared before them and offered his salutations by saying 'Hail! Hail! After exchanging courtesies they sat down together to have a discourse. Machhinder asked: 'Nanak! What is your experience with and how do you envision the world-ocean?' How did you swim across the sea?' Then Baba recited the *Sabad* in Rag Ramkali, M:1:

*Which is said to be the court, within which Thou sittest, O Lord? From amongst all the courts, who can see that court? Let someone come and tell me of the court, for the sight of which I go about sadly.1. In what way can I ferry across the world-ocean? I can die not, whilst alive.1. Pause. Pain is the door filled with filled with the two shutters hope and anxiety, and wrath is the guardsman. The water of worldly valuables is the moat. Within this water, man has built a house. After overcoming such difficulties, man sees the Lord, sitting in the seat of truth.2. How many Names hast Thou, O Lord? I know not their end. Equal to Thee, there is not another. Vociferate thou not and live within thy very mind. The Lord Himself knows and Himself does all.3. As long as there is desire, so long is there anxiety. How can then one speak of the One Lord? When in the midst of hopes, man remains without hope, then, O Nanak, meets he, the One Lord.4. In this way, the world-ocean is crossed. Like this one remains dead while alive.1. Pause 2nd.3. (SGGS 877)*

Then again Baba recited the *Sabad* in Rag Ramkali M:1:-

*The Lord's meditation and the Guru's instruction is the music of my horn, which the people hear. Honour is my bowl for begging, and I long to have the alms of the Lord's Name.1. O father God! The Protector of the Universe, ever remains wakeful. Ho alone is Gorakh, who is containing the world, and who made no delay in fashioning it.1. Pause. Binding together water, air etc, the Lord has placed life in the body and made the great lamps of the moon and the sun. To die and to live, God has given us the earth, but so many favours of His, we have forgotten.2. There are good many adepts, strivers, yogis, wandering saints, spiritual guides and good men. If I meet them, then shall I utter the Lord's praise and then alone will say my mind serve Him.3. Paper and salt remain safe sound in clarified butter, and the lotus remains unaffected in water. What can death do unto them, O slave Nanak, who meet with such saints? 4.4. (SGGS 877)*

Machhinder spoke: 'Nanak! Adopt yoga so that you may be physically strong and remain safe from uncertainties and vicissitudes of this world. By adopting Yoga, you may be able to easily cross over the dreadful ocean.' Guru Baba recited the *Sabad* in Rag Ramkali M:1 :-

*Says Nanak, hear thou, O Machhinder! He, who subdues the five demons, wobbles not. He who practices 'Yog' in such a way, saves himself, and saves his whole lineage.1. He alone is the forsaker who has attained such an understanding. Day and night, he remains absorbed in profound trance.1. Pause. He begs for the devotional service of the Lord and abides in His fear. He is sated with the invaluable gift of contentment. Becoming the embodiment of the Lord's meditation, he attains to a seat of equilibrium. He fixes his mind's attention to the True Name.2. Nanak utters the Nectareal Gurbani. Hearken thou, o Machhinder, this is the insignia of a detached Yogi. He, who amidst hope, remains without hope, assuredly meets with his Creator.3. Supplicates Nanak, I utter to thee, the secret things and effect of the union of the Guru with his disciple. 4.5. (SGGS 877-878)*

Then Gorakh Nath entreated by saying: 'Spiritual chieftainship is your capital. It has been prevalent since ages.' The Baba replied: Who should I adopt as my Guru, Gorakh Nath?' He replied: 'Who could be such a being that could place his blessed hand upon your head? There is no one in this world that has the divine authority to do so. Only the person who emerges from your own physical 1self can be your Guru.' Then Baba said: 'All be well with you.' The Baba moved on with his journey. Thus concluded the discourse with Machhinder.

This narration was written by Saedo Jatt of caste Gheho. Say *Waheguru!*

# 47. Shivnabh, Pran Sangli

While moving on with their journey, Baba along with his companion thought of going to Singhladeep. They travelled and stood in front of the unfathomable, unending sea. The Baba said: 'How shall we swim across, how shall we pass this unending sea?' The companions entreated, Saedo and Seeho said: 'O Master! By your order, even mountains swim.' Then Baba said: 'Come and he started reciting the following Saloka':-

*There is but One God. True is His Name; creative His personality and Immortal His form. He is without fear, sans enmity, unborn and self-illumined. By the Guru's grace (He is obtained).*

The Baba ordained: 'Whoever shall recite this *Saloka* with a pious heart along with true devotion and anyone that may listen to it, shall cross over the dreadful sea.' Then the devotees fell at Baba's feet, and said: 'O Master! Whoever you may be pleased with, your blessings shall help them cross the mighty sea.' With the Divine's grace, they easily maneuvered over the vast sea.

The Baba went to Singhladeep which was ruled by King Shivnabh. He stayed at the King's garden located near sea. The garden was called *Naulakha* and belonged to Shivnabh. It had been barren, lifeless for many years. As soon as Guru Nanak arrived there, it became lush and green. Fruit trees got laden with flowers and fruits. As the gardener, Maghore saw the miracle, he could not believe his eyes. The garden had been laying waste since ages and now it had become green and was flourishing. He was utterly surprised and overjoyed. He ran over and gave the good news to King Shivnabh. He exclaimed: 'O Master! Come outside. By virtue of the presence of a *Faqir*, the garden has become all green'. Then Raja Shivnabh called forth his beautiful maids and sent them to the garden to test whether the *Faqir* was indeed a genuine, holy person.

The alluring maids started dancing and merrymaking there and tried to allure Guru Nanak. They presented various shows of amusement; however, the Baba uttered not a word as he remained in his meditation. Having failed at alluring the Guru, the maids went to the Raja and narrated to him their experience. Soon after, Raja Shivnabh came over and inquired: 'O holy man! What is your name? What is your caste? Are you some yogi? Be gracious and come inside the palace'. The Baba recited the following *Sabad* in Rag Maru M;

*The Yogi, who is attached to the Lord's Name is pure. To him, not even a particle of filth sticks. The Beloved, True Lord, he even deems to be with him and his state of coming and going is ended. 1. O Lord of the Universe! What is Thy Name like and how is it known? If Thou callest me into Thy presence, I would ask Thee one thing, as to how can the mortal become one with Thee?* **Pause.**

The Raja asked: 'Are you Brahmin'? Then Baba recited the second Pauri:-

*He alone is a Brahmin, who bathes in the God's gnosis and who has God's praise for his leaves of worship. There is but One Name, One Pervading God and the One Light in the three worlds. 2.*

The Raja asked again: 'O Sir! Are you Khatri'? Then Baba recited the third Pauri:-

*Making my tongue the beam and this mind the pan of the scale, I weigh the inestimable Name. There is but One shop and One Supreme Merchant above all. All the petty dealers deal in the same sort of commodity. 3. At both the ends, the True Guru saves. He alone understands it, who is attuned to the One Lord and whose mind is free from doubt. He, whoever serves his Lord, day and night, ends doubt and abides the Name in his mind.4.*

Raja Shivnabh asked: 'O Sir! Are you Gorakh Nath'? The Baba recited the fifth Pauri: -

*High above is the sky, above the sky is God, the Protector of the world and the Unfathomable Great Lord of that world abides there. By Guru's instruction, abroad and home, deem I alike. Nanak has become such an anchoret.5.11. (SGGS 992)*

When Guru Baba concluded his reciting, the Raja came to know that he was an authentic Guru, the one he was looking for and meditating upon. He immediately fell at his feet. He requested, and said: 'Be gracious, and let's go home'. The Baba said: 'I don't go on foot.' Then Raja Shivnabh said: 'O Master! Everything blessed by you is here. If you order, you may ride a horse or an elephant, or even a chariot.' The Guru Baba said: 'Whatever it may be, O Raja! I only ride a human being.' The Raja said: 'O Master! We have many men. Do ride and come.' The Baba said: 'O Raja! The man must be a royal prince and be the town's king and on his back I shall ride.' Then the Raja said: 'O Royal Master! I am the Raja bestowed by you. Please ride on my back and let's go.' The Baba climbed on the Raja's back. On seeing this, the inhabitants of the city started saying: 'The Raja has gone mad.' Meanwhile, the Baba sat calmly while he was being carried by the King.

Later on, Queen Chandarkala and Raja Shivnabh stood before the Baba with folded hands and requested: 'please let us know what you would like to eat.' The Baba said: 'I'm on fast today.' Then Raja Shivnabh said: 'Can we offer you any type of food, Master?' The Guru Baba replied: 'I would like to eat meat prepared from a human's flesh.' Raja Shivnabh said: 'By your grace Master, many men are available.' The Baba said: 'O Raja! The man must be a son who has been born into a Raja's house and is royal prince of twelve years. His flesh shall make my food'.

The Raja and Queen became alarmed at this strange request. The Raja said: 'O Lord! Will it be alright if I bring a son from another Raja's house?' The Queen said: 'How shall one comply with this request. You better have a battle with the King and if you win, you shall get our son.' The Queen said: 'O Raja! We have only one son. Better look at his horoscope'.

The priests read the prince's horoscope and concluded that he would only live up till the age of twelve years. Then the Raja said: 'O son! Your body has been requested by the Guru; what are your thoughts?' The boy said: 'O father! What more can be better than this? My body shall be of use to the Guru.' The Raja said: 'He has been married for eight days. It is better to ask his wife also.' Then the Raja and Queen went and sat beside their daughter-in-law. The Raja said: 'O daughter! The body of your husband shall be consumed by the Guru; what is your opinion?' The girl spoke: O father! His body will be liberated by the Guru and my widowhood will appease and satisfy him. There is nothing else better than this.'

Shortly after, all four came and stood before the Guru. Raja Shivnabh spoke: 'O Master! The boy is present here before you.' Then Baba said: 'He is not of any use to me in the current form. Ask his mother to hold his arms and his wife to hold his feet and you, with a knife in your hand must sacrifice him. I shall receive satisfaction only then.'

Raja Shivnabh obeyed the Guru's order and taking a knife in his hand, he sacrificed the boy. The body was cooked and placed before the Guru. The Baba said: 'The three of you must shut your eyes, say *Waheguru* and put the food into your mouth.' The Raja, Queen and daughter-in-law closed their eyes and put the cooked body into their mouth while saying *Waheguru*; all lfour were sitting together. However, when they opened their eyes, Guru Baba was not present anymore.

On not seeing the Guru and due to the loss of his son, the Raja became emotionally unstable and went to the garden. He was wearing wooden sandals on his feet and was bare-headed. He walked up and down while repeating 'Guru, Guru'. After twelve months, the Baba came back and blessed them. Guru Nanak explained that birth and death is a circle of life and one must accept this fact. Shivnabh listened to the Guru's sermon and was emancipated. He became a devout follower of Guru Nanak who accepted him as his obedient disciple.

The Raja was initiated to become a devotee of Guru Nanak by Saedo Jatt of caste Ghohe. Following their King's footsteps, the entire island of Singhladeep became Guru Nanak's disciples and started repeating 'Guru, Guru'. The region was liberated by virtue of Shivnabh's unselfish and devotional conduct. Everyone say *Waheguru*!

*Rahuras* (evening prayer) was recited by the congregation of Singhladeep. When night fell, the entire population of the island gathered and sat together in the *Dharamsala*. During this time, a devotee prepared food for the assembled congregation. Enormous quantity of food had to be prepared because of the size of the gathering. As much as twenty one *maunds* of salt was used to prepare the entire meal. The next day everyone gathered and had the food to their heart's content. At that location, Guru Nanak's mysterious hymns were revealed. They are in the form of Pran Sanghli (sermon of the non-existent). The Baba manifested this Granth while he was in deep meditation and thinking of *Nirankar* (Formless).

At the island, the Granth is known as Guru's Pran Sanghli. Discrete discussions had taken place regarding the **3**physical self; however, no one could scribe the message in a written form and the original Granth was left there. In later years, Saedo and Gheho undertook to have it written, near Gorakh Harti. One chowk, about two *Kos* away exists near Gorakh Hatri. It is four *Kos* away from the cremation memorial where he started living unattached. It was forecast that a devotee from Punjab would come to the island in the foreseeable future to view and take away the Granth. Guru Nanak had bestowed his blessings upon Shivnabh. Everyone say *Waheguru*!

# 48. Baadhi's Hut Demolished

Guru Nanak came over and stayed with a person named Badhi. He offered utmost regard, respect and service to the Guru. He spread a cot out for him to relax after his long journey.

Baba slept the whole night there and next day, he removed a wooden piece that was holding the hut together. He struck the cot with it and broke it. He then went outside after breaking Badhi's bed. Seeing this unusual behavior of the Guru, Saedo asked: 'O Master! No one offered space to us in this town and this Baadhi gave us a place to stay. You have destroyed the cot he offered us. This poor fellow had only one hut and a cot. Both of these possessions have now been ravaged by you. What will happen to him now?'

The Baba explained: 'Saedo! His service and regard has been well-accorded.' As Baadhi went home, he saw that the four bed-posts of his cot were sunk in the earth and underneath it was buried treasures, including gemstones all around. The poor man was able to retrieve the hidden treasure and built a palace at the spot where his hut was once located. Hearing this, Saedo and Seeho fell at Baba's feet. They then came home, stayed for a few days and then moved further on.

# Third Udasi – The Third Travelogue

## 49. Third Udasi - Kashmir - Brahm Das Pandit

Third *Udasi* (the third Travelogue) this journey involved Guru Nanak's travels to the Northern region. During this part of his travelogue and for his daily sustenance, the Baba ate the split parts along with Akk flowers (which is a wild plant). He consumed these after drying out their moisture. To cover his body, he used leather wrapping, wore leather sandals on his feet and tied a leather covering over his head. On his forehead, he put a mark of saffron. During this part of the journey, two individuals: Hasu Lohar and Seehan Chhimba accompanied him.

Guru Nanak after travelling for some days reached Kashmir and stayed there for a short while. Inhabitants of the land came and paid a visit to him and after listening to his sermons, became his Name-devotees. There lived a person by the name of Pandit Brahm Das* of Kashmir. He had heard 'that a *Faqir* had come over and was residing nearby.' The Pandit had a habit of carrying two camel loads of *religious books* wherever he went and wore an idol of a deity around his neck. He came to see the Guru, offered greetings, and sat down near him. On seeing the unusual clothing worn by the Guru, he inquired: 'What sort of *sadhu* are you! Why have you worn leather? Why have you wrapped yourself with ropes? And why have you left your worldly life? Why do you shun fish and meat?' The Baba recited the following in *Rag Malar*, the *Vaar* of the Guru:-

**Salok Mehla 3.** *On meeting the Guru, the soul blossoms, as, the earth is embellished after the bursting forth of the cloud. Everything appears green and the ponds and the tanks are filled to the brim. The love of the True Lord attached to the mind as redness to the madder. Obeying the True Lord, the heart lotus blooms and one is rendered happy, through the Guru's word. The wayward person is on the other side of God. Ascertain thou this by seeing with thy eyes. Like the deer ensnared in the net, the death's courier is seen standing over his head. Vile are hunger, thirst and slander and terrible are lust and wrath. Until one reflects not on the Guru's word, one sees not the Lord with these eyes. Whoever is pleasing to Thee, O Lord, he becomes content and his domestic involvements are past. Serving the Guru, man's capital is saved. The Guru is the ladder and the boat of salvation.*

*Nanak, whoever is attached to the Lord, he receives His quintessence. Thou, O True Lord, art attained through the true mind.1. Mehla 1. There is but one road and one door. The Guru is the ladder to reach one's own place. Beauteous is the Lord, O Nanak. All the comforts are in the True Name.2. Pauri. Of Himself, the Lord created Himself, and He alone knows Himself. Separating the sky and the earth, He has spread the canopy of the firmament. Making His command manifest, the Lord has supported the sky without pillars. Creating the sun and the moon, the Lord infused His light within them. He created the night and day. Wondrous are His wondrous plays. The Lord created the places of pilgrimage, where the mortals reflect upon goodness and bathe on the auspicious occasions. Equal to Thee, there is not another, O Lord. How can I describe and narrate Thee? Thou art seated on the External Throne, All others but come and go.1. Salok Mehla 1. Nanak, if it rains in the month of Sawan, the four things feel great joy. They are the serpent, the deer, the fish and the revelers who have wealth in their home.1. M:1. Nanak, if it rains in the month of Sawan, the four things suffer separation. They are the cow's calves, the poor, the way-farers and the servants. Pauri. O True Lord, True art Thou, who dispenseth nothing but Truth. The lotus-like, Thou sittest in trance and art hid from the eyes. Brahma is called great, but he too knows not Thy limit. He has no father, nor a mother who has begotten Thee, O my Lord. He has neither the form, nor the sign. Of all the castes, He has none. He has no hunger and thirst and is sated and satiated. The Lord has merged His ownself in the Guru through whom dispenses He His Name. By pleasing the true Lord, the mortal merges in True Lord.2. (SGGS 1278-1279)*

The *Vaar* of Malar 27 concluded and Pandit Brahm Das reverently came near, offered his obeisance at Baba's feet and said: 'O Master! Before this world existed, where was God?' Then Baba recited the *Sabad* in Rag *Maru Solha* M: 1.

*For countless ages, there was utter darkness. There was no earth and no sky, but the Infinite Lord's will alone was pervasive. There was neither day, nor night, nor moon, nor sun, but the Lord alone sat in profound trance.1. Neither there were mines of creation, nor speech, nor air, nor water. Neither creation, nor destruction, nor coming, nor going was there. There were no continents, nor underworlds, nor seven oceans, nor rivers and nor the flowing of water.2. Then there was no higher, middle and lower plane. Neither there was hell, nor heaven, nor death, nor time. There was no world of torture or region of bliss; no birth or death, nor did any come or go.3. There was no Brahma, nor Vishnu or Shiva. None else was seen but He, the One Lord. neither there was female, nor male, nor caste nor birth nor did anyone suffer pain or pleasure.4. Then there was neither the celibate, nor the man of charity, nor the forest-dweller. Then there was no adept, no striver, and no dweller at ease. There was no Yogi, a wandering sage and the religious garb and none called himself the supreme Yogi.5. There was no contemplation, penance, self-control, fasting and worship. Nor did anyone speak or tell of duality. Creating His ownself, the Lord was supremely rejoiced and Himself valued His Ownself.6. There was no purification, or self-restraint, or rosary of sweet basil. There was no milkmaid, or Krishan, or cow or herdsman. There were no incantations and spells, no hypocrisy, nor did any one play on the flute.7. There were no deeds, religion and the gadfly of mammon. Caste and birth were not to be seen with eyes, There was no noose of secular attachment, nor was death writ on the mortal's brow, nor did anyone meditate on aught else.8. There was no slender, no seed, no soul and no life. Then there was no Gorakh or Machhinder. Then there was no Divine knowledge, meditation, lineage and creation, nor any reckoning of accounts.9. There was no caste, or religious garb, or Brahmin or Khatri. Neither there was demigod, nor temple, nor cow, nor the Hindu's primal spell. There used to be no burnt offerings, nor gratuitous feasts, nor ablutions at holies, and nor did any one perform worship.10. There was no Musim scholar or judge. There used to be no Muslim preacher, nor a penitent nor Mecca-pilgrim. There was no subject, king and worldly pride, nor did any one give himself a big Name.11. There was no love or devotion, nor mind or matter. There used to be no friend, intimate, seed and blood. The Lord Himself was the Banker and Himself the Merchant. Such was the will of the True Lord.12. There existed no Vedas, nor Muslim books, nor Simritis and nor Shastras. There was no reading of Puranas, nor sun-rise, nor sunset. The Incomprehensible Lord was Himself the Speaker and Preacher. The Unseeable Lord Himself saw everything.13. When He so willed, then created He the world and without support sustained the firmament. He created Brahma, Vishnu and Shiva and extended the love of mammon.14. Rare is the person whom the Guru causes to hear the Lord's word. By His will, the Lord has created the creation and watches over all. He founded the continents, solar systems and underworlds and from the absolute self, He became manifest.15. His limit no one knows. It is through the Perfect Guru, that I have obtained understanding.*

*Nanak, wondrous art they, who are imbued with the Lord's truth and hymning His praise they become delighted. 16.3.15. (SGGS 1035-1036)*

Pandit Brahm Das comprehended the divine message imparted by Guru Nanak, felt invigorated and offered reverence by kneeling down before Baba's feet. He threw away the stone idol from his neck and became Name-devotee of the Baba. He started serving the Guru; however, his mind remained restless, his ego ceased to vanish and he still thought of himself as all-knowing and divine being. He kept on serving the Guru mechanically, without inner devotion, in a neutral equipoise. A thought did linger in his mind that he had performed similar service before and even while serving Guru Nanak, he did not feel content. Meanwhile, the Guru was able to see through the Pandit's apprehension and felt that he needed to be taught a lesson.

One day he asked the Pandit: 'Go, and adopt some other Guru.' Then Pandit asked: 'Who should I adopt as Guru?' Guru Baba replied: 'As you go beyond, there is a room in the garden. Four *Faqirs* are sitting there. They will tell you.' Then Brahm Das left from there. He went and offered his obeisance to the Faqirs. Shortly, after having a nap for a part of an hour, the mendicants said: 'There is your Guru in that *temple.' The Pandit eagerly went over to the direction of the sanctuary and offered his regards to the person seated there. He saw a woman wearing pink clothes, standing and waiting for him in the temple. As the Pandit approached her, she took off her footwear and struck him with it. He ran back frightened and laminated of his misgiving. On seeing him running towards them, the Faqirs asked 'did you see the Guru?' The Pandit revealed the entire episode and asked why he had been battered by her. After listening to him, the Faqirs said: 'O Brother! She was the form of worldly illusion (*maya*) and of which you had the temptation, the desire to possess. You had the perfect being as your Guru, yet you left him to seek another.' The Pandit realized his mistake, returned home and fell at Baba's feet. He threw away his two camel-loads of *religious books*. He started repeating 'Guru, Guru'. He became humble devotee of the congregation. Say all *Waheguru*!

Hasu Lohar and Seehae Chhimba wrote the Bani. The Baba recited the following *Saloka*:-

*Salok Mehla 1. With the award of the punishment of the thousand marks of vulva, Indar did weep. Paras Ram returned home crying. Ajai wailed, when made to eat the dung he gave in charity. Such is the punishment, meted out in God's court. Rama wept when he was exiled and got separated from Sita and Lachhman. Ten-headed Ravana, who took away Sita with the beat of tambourine, wept, when he lost Ceylon. The Pandvas who's Master lived with them, became servants and wailed. Janmeja wailed that he went astray. For an offence, he became a sinner. The Divine teachers, seers and religious guides weep, lest they should suffer agony at the last moment. The kings weep, having their ears torn and they go abegging from house to house. The miser weeps when his amassed wealth parts company with him. The learned man cries when his learning fails him. The young woman weeps for she has no husband. Nanak, the whole world is in distress. He, who believes in the Name, becomes victorious. No other deed is of any account.1. (SGGS 953-954)*

The Baba felt pleased and he moved further on.

## 50. Discourse with *Sidhas* at Sumeir and Achal

Guru Nanak went on with his travels and after crossing over one and a quarter lakh mountains, reached the summit the of Sumeir. There was a 1spot related to Mahadev at this location. Further ahead were sitting: 2Mahadeo, Gorakh Nath, Bharthari, Gopi Chand and Charpat. Baba. On reaching there, the Guru offered greetings to all of them and sat down nearby. Then the *Sidhas* gave him a vessel and said: 'Go and bring it back filled* with water, O son of Kalyuga!' The Baba went to fill* the vessel. He put the vessel in water* and to his surprise diamonds and pearls filled the container. Guru Baba struck the canister against the earth which shattered it into pieces. Thereafter, the Baba restored the pot by putting together the pieces and recited the *Saloka:-*

*He only is the breaker, designer and fashioner, and nothing but the truth, says Nanak, does exist. (Not in SGGS)*

After reciting the holy words, the mystical charms ceased to exhibit their magical powers and the vessel ultimately filled with simple water. It was brought over to the *Sidhas* and all of them drank from it to their heart's content; however, even after everyone drank from it, the canister remained full of water. Thereafter, Mahadeo asked: 'Are you a family man or a recluse?' Then Baba replied: 'what traits relate to an *Udasi* (recluse) and what traits does a family man *have?' Then Mahadeo spoke:-

*He alone is the house-holder, who checks his passions and begs from the Lord meditation, hard toil and self-restraint. He, who with his body gives in charity and alms all he can; that house-holder is pure like the Ganges water. Says Nank, hear thou, O Ishar, the Lord is the Embodiment of truth. 2. (SGGS 952)*

Then Guru Baba responded:-

*M:1. How is sin eradicated? How is the way to real life found? What is the use of taking food by having the ears torn? It is the One Name, that eternally inheres, both when the universe is in existence and non-existence. Which is the word, whereby the mind remains steady? If man endures sun-shine (peace) and shade (pain) alike, then alone, says Nanak, he can utter the Name of the Great Lord. Becoming disciples, people engage themselves in the six systems. They are neither the true worldly men, nor the true forsakers of the world. He who remains absorbed in the Formless Lord, why goes he to beg alms?.7.(SGGS 953)*

Gopi Chand who was an *Udasi* spoke about the traits of an *Udasi*:-

*M:1. He alone is the renunciator, who embraces renunciation. He realizes the Immaculate Lord, abiding in the lower and upper regions. He gathers the moon of coolness and the sun of gnosis. Of that renunciator, the body-wall falls not. Says Nanak, hear thou, O Gopi Chand, the Lord is the Embodiment of truth. The Supreme Reality has no sign or form.4.( SGGS 952)*

The Baba replied:- (See appendix 4, Part 1).

Gorakh Nath who was a Yogi spoke about the traits of a Yogi.

*M: 1. He alone is detached, who burns his self-conceit. The hard-toil, he makes his food obtained through begging. He, who asks for alms to the town of his mind; that farsaker mounts to the Lord's city. Says Nanak, hear thou, O Gorakh, the Lord is the Embodiment of truth. The Supreme Reality has neither sign nor form.5. . (SGGS 952)*

The Guru Baba responded: (See appendix 4, Part 2).

Charpat who was a Yogi spoke about the traits of a Yogi.

*Salok. He alone is the disguiser, who washes off his body's filth. His body's fire, he burns in the Lord's Name. Even in dream, he emits not his seed. Such a disguiser ages not, nor dies he. Says Nanak, hear, O Charpat, the Lord is the Embodiment of truth. The Supreme Reality has no sign and form.(SGGS 953)*

The Guru spoke:- (**See appendix 4, Part 3**).

Bharthari who was an ascetic spoke about the traits of this sect:-

*Salok. He alone is desireless, who turns towards the Lord. God, the Pillar, he fixes in his tenth gate. Night and day, he remains absorbed in hearty meditation. Such a desireless person is like the True Lord. Says Nanak, hear thou, O Bharthar, the Lord is the Embodiment of truth. The Supreme Reality has no sign and form.* (SGGS 953)

Then Guru Baba responded:- (**See appendix 4, Part 4**).

Then Bharthari said: 'You should become a Yogi and live for ages.'

The Baba said: 'What form does Yoga belong to?'

Bharthari spoke of the form of Yoga: *With ear-rings, patched coat, begging lap and a sectarian staff, and the horn's sound to produce divine music resounding the universe over.*

The Baba recited the following *Sabad* in Rag Asa:-

**Asa Mehla 1.** *The Guru's word is the ear-rings in my mind, and wears I the patched coat of forbearance. Whatever the Lord does, I consider that as good, and thus easily obtain I the treasure of Yog.1. O father, the soul thus united is a Yogi, all the ages through, and it is absorbed in the Supreme quintessence. He, who has obtained the ambrosial Name of the Immaculate Lord, his body enjoys the pleasure of Divine Knowledge.1. Pause. He forsakes desire and disputes and sits in contemplative mood in the Lord's city (audience). From the horn's sound, an everlasting and beautiful melody is produced which, day and night, fills him with Divine music.2. Reflection is the cup, Divine Knowledge his sectarian staff and to abide in Lord's presence is his ashes. God's praise is my vocation, and the Exalted Guru's way is my pure religion.3.. Mine arms' support is to see Lord's light amongst all, and it has various and many colours. Says Nanak, listen thou, O Bharthari Yogi. I profess love only for the Supreme Lord.4.3.37. (SGGS 359-360)*

Afterwards, the Sidhas said: 'Nanak! You should reach 3Achal. A fair is held there and you can get a glimpse of other Sidhas.' The Baba replied: 'How many days does it take to get to Achal?' The *Sidhas* replied: 'Nanak! Achal is a distance of three days from here. We have the powers to get there at the speed of wind.' Baba replied: 'You proceed on. We shall come at a slower speed.' Then the *Sidhas* started on their journey and left Guru Nanak. After bidding farewell to them, Baba closed his eyes and as the mind can travel anywhere in an instant, he used his psyche abilities and after concentrating his thoughts towards the destination, opened his eyes and arrived at Achal within mere seconds. He then went and sat under a *bohr*. Shortly after, the *Sidhas* too reached the destination. They were surprised to see Nanak already seated there, ahead of them. The *Sidhas* inquired: 'For how long have you been here?' The other Sidhas nearby responded: 'Today is his third day of his arrival.' The *Sidhas* felt surprised and astonished.

After a while everyone decided to have a drink to quench their thirst. They started passing around a flask filled with a solution. It was eventually brought over to Guru Nanak. On seeing it, he asked: 'What is this?' The *Sidhas* said: 'This is a drink of the *Sidhas* and it has been made from jiggery and the flowers of 4basia-latifolia.'

The Baba spoke the *Sabad* in Rag Asa M:1:-

*Make gnosis thy molasses and meditation thine flowers of basia-latifolia, and in them put the doing of good actions as thy fermenting bark. Make faith thy furnace and love thy plaster and in this way the sweet Nectar is distilled.1. O Sire, by quaffing the Name-Nectar, the mind becomes intoxicated and easily remains absorbed in Lord's love. By fixing attention on God's affection and hearing celestial strain, day and night, become fruitful.1. Pause. The Perfect One, in a natural way, gives this cup of truth to drink to him, on whom He casts His merciful glance. Why should he, who is the dealer of Nectar, cherish love for paltry wine?2. The Guru's word is a nectar-speech and by quaffing it, man becomes acceptable. What should he, who is the lover of Lord's court and sight, do with salvation and paradise?3. He, who is imbued with God's praise, is ever a renouncer and loses not his life in gamble. Says Nanak, hear O Bharthari Yogi, I am intoxicated with the ambrosial stream of Name.4.4.38. (SGGS 360)*

After hearing the Sabad from Guru Nanak, the *Sidhas* offered their salutations. The Baba ordained: 'all salutations must be offered to the Lord Primal'!* Soon after, the Baba set forth from there. Say all *Waheguru*!

**Fourth *Udasi* - Fourth Travelogue**

# 51. Fourth *Udasi* towards West, Mecca

Fourth *Udasi* was undertaken towards the Western direction.

Guru Nanak proceeded on his journey. This time he wore footwear and undergarments made of leather. He displayed a rosary made of bones around his neck and put a mark on his forehead. His clothes were of colour blue. While on his way, he played along with the young ones and enjoyed their innocent, juvenile company. As this went on, he came near a caravan of devotees proceeding for the Hajj. Soon after, a Qazi met him, and they stayed together and talked during the night. Then the Haji asked: 'O dervish! You don't have any bowl, wooden staff or any hemp-like intoxicant. Are you a Hindu or Musalman?' Then Baba recited the *Sabad* in Rag Tilang, M:1:-

*O Lord, Thy fear is my hemp and my mind is the leather pouch. I have become an intox-icated hermit. My hands are the begging bowl and I crave for Thine vision, O God. Day by day, beg I at Thy door.1. For Thy sight, I make a mumper's call. Bless Thou me, Thine door's beggar, with alms, O Lord.1. Pause. Saffron, flowers, deer's musk and gold embel-lish all, the bodies. Like Chandan, such is the quality of Lord's slaves that they render fragrant one and all.2. No one calls clarified butter and silk polluted. Such is the saint, be he of high or low caste. They who make obeisance unto Thy Name and remain absorbed in Thy love, O Nanak, I beg at their door for alms.3.1.2. (SGGS 721)*

Then again the Hajji asked: 'O Master! We live in this world. What shall become of us?' Then Baba recited the *Sabad* in Rag Tilang M:1:-

*Infusing His light into the dust, the Lord has made the universe and the world. The sky, earth, trees and water are the Lord's creation.1. O man, whatever the eye sees, is perish-able. The world is an eater of carrion, neglected of God and avaricious. Pause. Like a ghost and a beast, the world kills the forbidden and eats the carrion. Restrain thy heart, other-wise seizing thee, the Omnipotent Lord shall punish thee in hell.2. The patrons, dainties, brothers, courts, lands and homes. Tell me, of what avail shall these be to thee then, when Azrail, the death's myrmidon seizes thee?3. My Immaculate Lord knows thy condition. O Nanak, say thy prayer to the pious persons to lead thee to the right path.4.1. (SGGS 723)*

Then Baba bade his farewell to the people of the caravan and moved on from there and headed towards Mecca. He was accompanied by a person with the intention of performing

Hajj. While they were walking, there appeared a miniature shred of cloud over their head. The Hajji saw it and felt disturbed; he thought that it may be a bad omen and said: 'This cloudlet is upon me.' A thought came to his mind that since he was being accompanied by a Non-Muslim, it may cause him bad luck. He remonstrated to the Baba: 'no Hindu has ever gone to Mecca; you should not come along with me. He told Guru Nanak to leave his company and either go ahead of him or behind him.' The Baba said: 'Be it all well. You walk ahead.' The man started walking ahead. After a short while, as he looked back, the Baba nor the small patch of cloud was following him. Then the Hajji realized his mistake and started beating his hands in remorse. He said that God's impression had appeared before him; however, he could not comprehend his divine presence, he seemed to have been beguiled.'

Meanwhile, the Baba entered Mecca. There it had been ordained and written in books that 'one Nanak dervish would come and water would then appear in the well of the city.' Shortly afterwards Baba entered 1Mecca and fell asleep. He slept with his feet towards the holy structure at Mecca. Soon it was time for *Namaz*. A person by the name of Qazi Rukandeen came to offer his *Namaz*. He saw Nanak and said: 'O man of God! You have placed your feet towards Lord's house and towards Qaba; why have you done that?' The Baba replied: 'Drag my feet to whichever direction where God and Qaba does not reside.' Qazi Rukandeen slided Baba's feet towards the other direction. To his astonishment, wherever he moved Baba's feet, the Qaba moved towards that direction. After seeing this miracle, Qazi Rukandeen was wonderstruck and realized that he was in the company of a divine being. He kissed the feet of Guru Nanak and said: O dervish! What is your name?' Then Baba recited the following *Sabad* in Rag Tilang M:1.

*Own to practice fasting and meditation. Realising the ten physical inlets and dying even be ever sustained in pensive state. Pause. Subdue the mind and set right the vision and be ever engaged in pursuit of argumentation. Be ever imbued all the thirty days in such a state to be pure and being gentle and emanable to learning. You undergo fasting of conscience and happily renounce dancing. Keep the mental state ever in view and uphold chastity. Renounce taste as useless to tongue and renders the mind dubious and gloomy. Have Lord's mercy in mind and renounce vanity and disbelief. Extinguish the wave of lust on mind and be ever chill-cold. Do observe fasting, says Nanak, and keep patience to eternalize the act. (Not in SGGS)*

When Baba concluded recitation of the Sabad, Qazi Rukandeen offered his greetings and said: 'All applauds in wonder! We have had a glimpse of God's dervish.' Then he went to Pir Patlia2 and said: 'Nanak dervish has come'. Patlia Pir came to meet him and offered greetings to Guru Nanak. Both of them exchanged courtesies and sat down. They started applauding God. Then Qazi Rukandeen asked: 'O Master! They who read these 'Tees Haraf', do they receive anything worthwhile from it or are they doing lip service?' Then Baba spoke and gave a detailed explanation. A discourse took place with Qazi Rukandeen. Baba spoke in Rag Tilang M:1. Sheikh Rukandeen was then Qazi of Mecca. Baba spoke:-**3**

Then Qazi Rukandeen spoke: 'O Nanak dervish! These Hindus and Muslims who read Veidas and Puranas, will they attain God or not?' Then Baba recited the *Sabad* in Rag Tilang M:1:- **4**

*The Vedas and the four Semitic scriptures is unnecessary, O brother, if the mind's anxiety is not removed. If thou fix thy mind on God, even for a moment, then the Lord shall be seen just present before thee.1. O man, search thy heart and wander not in perplexity. This world is a magic show. In it there is no one to hold thy hand.1.* **Pause.** *Reading and reading falsehood, the mortals are delighted and being ignorant, talk non-sense. My Just True Creator is within His creation. He is not the Krishna of black form.2. In the tenth gate flows the stream of celestial bliss. Thou ought to have taken a bath in it. Ever perform thou the Lord's service. Wear these spectacles and see Him present everywhere.3. The Lord is the purest of the pure. Thou mayest entertain a doubt if there be another. Kabir, mercy wells up from the Merciful Lord. He alone knows, who does all this.4.1. (SGGS 727)*

Then Qazi Rukandeen said: 'Some people don't even read these and they commit ill-deeds. They never follow *roza* (fasting) or offer *Namaz* (Muslim Prayer). They drink wine and take hemp and poppy too. What will happen of them on the day of judgment?' Then Baba said:-

*Says Nanak, hear thou, O man, the true instruction. Seated in judgement and taking out His ledger, God shall call thee to account. The rebels of the Lord, with outstanding against them, shall be called out. The death's courier, Azrail, shall be appointed to punish them. Entangled in the narrow lane, they shall see no way of escape of coming and going. Falsehood shall come to an end, O Nanak, and truth shall ultimately prevail.2 . (SGGS 953)*

Then the Pir Patlia said: 'We are standing at this holy site of the world. How shall God stand as our surety?' Then Baba recited the *Sabad* in Rag Tilang M:1:-

*I utter one supplication before Thee. Hear it Thou, O my Creator. Thou art the true, great, merciful and faultless cherisher.1. The world is a perishable place. Know it for certain in thy mind, O man. Azrail, the death's courier, has caught me by the hair of my head, yet I know it not in the least, in my heart.1. Pause. The wife, son, father and brothers, no one shall hold my hand. At last when I fall and the time of last prayer is reached, there shall be no one to rescue me.2. Night and day, I wander in avarice and think of doing evil. I do not, ever, do good deeds. Like this is my condition.3. I am unfortunate as also miserly, negligent, shameless and without Thine fear, O Lord, Says Nanak, I am Thy slave and the dust of the feet of Thine servants 4.1.. (SGGS 721)*

After Baba recited this *Sabad*, Qazi Rukandeen and Pir Patlia came and offered their greetings and reverence. They kissed Baba's feet and by saying 'Waheguru' water emerged in the well. Baba felt satisfied and left from there and went home. Say all *Waheguru!*

**Fifth *Udasi* - Fifth Travelogue**

# 52. *Udasi*, the fifth; Discourse with the Sidhas

Fifth *Udasi*, the final journey of Guru Nanak. During his travels, the Baba reached *Gorakh Hatri*. The *Sidhas* saw him there and they started inquiring: 'So which *Khatri* are you?' Then Baba replied: 'They call me Nanak'. Eighty four *Sidhas* sat around in their yogic postures and then the *Sidhas* said: 'O good man! Say some wise words.' Then Baba spoke: Sri Satgurparsad. Goast M:1, Sidh Goast took place in Rag Ramkali:-

*The men of miracles forming an assembly sat on their seats and said to the Guru, "Make thou salutation to this assembly of saints". Answers the Guru: My salutation is unto Him, who is True, Infinite and extremely Exquisite. I cut off my head and lay it before Him and surrender my body and soul unto Him. Nanak, by meeting the Saint Guru, the True Lord is obtained and one is spontaneously blessed with glory.1. What is the good of wandering about? It is through the True Name that the man is rendered pure. Without the True Name, no one is emancipated. Q.1: "What art thou"? Q.2: What is thy Name"? Q. 3: What is thy sect"? Q. 4: What is thine life-object"? Our prayer is that thou tell us the truth. We are a sacrifice unto the pious persons. Q. 5: "Where is thy seat"? Q. 6: "Where abidest thou, O boy"? Q. 7: "Whence hast thou come"? Q. 8: "Whither goest thou"? The detached Sidhas say, hear thou, O Nanak. Q. 9: "What is the way"? Says the Guru{- The Lord is within all the hearts. A. 5: In Him is my seat. A. 6: In Him is my abode. A. 3: I walk in the True Guru's will and this alone is my sect. A, 7: I have proceeded from God. A. 8: I shall go whither He shall direct me in His will. A. 2: My Name is Nanak. A. 1: I am ever an obeyer of God's order. A. 9: To be seated in the Imperishable Lord's contemplative mood is my way. A. 4: The attainment of such a transcendent comprehension is my life object. Knowing and recognizing myself by Guru's grace, I have merged in the Truest of the true. The Yogis say:- The world ocean is said to be impassable. Q. 10: "How can one cross it"? Charpat says:- "O Nanak, the detached, give thou a true reply after due deliberation". Nanak answers:- "He who says that he himself understands, what answer can I give him"? Truly speaking unto thee that how can I argue with thee when thou deemest that thou hast reached the yonder shore". A. 10: As a lotus flower remains unaffected in water, as also a duck swims against the stream's current and becomes not wet, so with fixed intent on the Guru's word and uttering the Name, O Nanak, the dreadful world-ocean is crossed. He who lives in an aloneness, enshrining the One Lord in his mind, living without desire in the midst of desires and sees and shows to others the Inaccessible and Incomprehensible Lord, of him Nanak is a slave". (SGGS 938)*

Pauri 73. After listening to Guru Nanak, the *Sidhas* offered a drinking cup of five seer to him; however, the Baba poured it down into the earth. The *Sidhas* became incensed at what they saw. They were offended that Guru Nanak would decline their offering and throw it away in an impolite manner. The *Sidhas* demanded: 'You show us a miracle, show anything within your power.' The Baba said: 'Please begin by displaying your divine powers and afterwards you will see mine.' Then the *Sidhas* started showing their esoteric powers and magical wonders. Someone made a dear skin fly. Someone threw up a heavy stone slab with his powers. Another exhaled fire out of his mouth, while the next one made a wall to move along as if it was running. On seeing this, the Baba went into an ecstasy and recited the *Sabad:-*

**Salok M: 1.** *If I put on the dress of fire, found a house in snow and make iron my food; all the troubles if I drink as water and drive before me the earth. By placing the firmament in the balance pan, were I to weigh it with a mere copper put in the hind pan; were I to* *become so large that I could nowhere be contained; and were I to snaffle and lead by the nose one and all. If I possess so much power within my mind that I perform and also at my bidding cause others to perform such things, but all this is in vain. As great as the Lord is, so great are His gifts. He bestows them according to His pleasure. Nanak, he on whom the Lord casts His merciful glance, obtains the glory of the True Name. (SGGS 147)*

On hearing this Sabad, the *Sidhas* felt their powers were subdued by Guru Nanak and humbly offered their greetings to him. The Baba spoke: 'Hail to the Primal Being.' Thereafter, Guru Nanak recited the *Sabad* in Rag Gauri, Ashatpadi M:1:-

*Gauri Mehla 5. Firstly, man issues from dwelling in the womb. Afterwards, he attaches himself to his sons, wife and family. The dishes of many sorts and varied dresses, shall, assuredly, pass away, O wretched man.1. Which is the place that never perishes? What word is that by which evil intellect is removed?1. Pause. In the realm of Indar, death is sure and certain. The realm of Brahma is not to remain permanent. The realm of Shiva shall do perish. The mammon with three qualities and the demons shall vanish.2. The mountain, trees, the earth, the sky and the stars, the sun, the moon, wind, fire and water, the day, the night, the fasting and their differentiation, the Shastras, the Simritis and the Vedas, all shall pass away.3. Places of pilgrimage, gods, temples and books, rosaries, frontal marks, the reflectives, the pure and the performers of burnt offerings, loin clothes, prostrations, provisions and revelments, all these things and all the men shall pass away.4. The castes, races, Musalmans and Hindus; the beasts, the birds, and sentient beings of various varieties; the entire world and the creation which comes to view, these all forms of existence shall perish.5. By Lord's praise, His devotional service and the real Divine Knowledge, man attains Eternal Bliss and immovable true seat. There, in the Saints' congregation, he lovingly sings Lord's praises. There, he ever abides in the fearless city.6. There is no fear, doubt, mourning and anxiety there. No coming, going, and death is there. There is for ever joy and theatre of spontaneous music there. The devoted slaves of God abide there, and singing of Lord's praises is their sustenance.7. Of the Supreme Lord, there is no end and limit. Who can embrace His contemplation? Says Nanak, he, to whom the Lord shows mercy, is delivered through the guild of Saints, and attains to the Imperishable Abode.8.4. (SGGS 237)*

The *Sidhas* offered their respects and said: 'Greetings! Greetings!' Then Baba replied: 'Greetings to the Primal Being.' After spending some time with them, the Guru Baba came back home.

# 53. Test of Sri Lehna; Maid Tulsan

As per the will of the Almighty divine God, there once lived a devotee whose caste was Bhalla in a town called Khadur. He would constantly contemplate on the Omnipotent and perpetually repeated 'Guru, Guru.' The residents of Khadur were the followers of goddess Durga and were unhappy with the devotee for not following their deity. This pious person lived near the vicinity of Trehans. The priest of this location was a person by the name of Lehna. One day, the pious devotee whose caste was Bhalla was in deep thought and was repeating the Guru's Name. Soon after, Guru Angad* heard of this recitation and felt enamored with the divine words. He inquired: 'Whose *Sabad* is this?' Then the pious man replied: 'This is Nanak's *Sabad*.' Then Guru Angad* had a desire to meet the Baba and accompanied the man and reached the abode of Guru Nanak. He came and fell at the Master's feet. On having a glimpse of the Holy Man, he broke off the tinkling bells tied to his hands and feet and started repeating Guru's Name. He would come daily in the presence of Guru Nanak. He would devotedly serve him, clean his utensils and waved a fan at him.

On one occasion, late at night, after performing his daily service to the Baba, Guru Angad saw a woman wearing purple clothes. She was reverently sitting nearby and had an aura of light emanating from her. Seeing her, Guru Angad implored: 'O Master! Who was she, O Lord?' The Baba replied: 'O Angad! She was Durga. She comes to serve the Guru every eighth day.' On hearing this, Guru Angad* immediately fell at the Baba's feet.

One day, Guru Angad was massaging the Guru's feet. To his surprise, he saw numerous creatures dispensing from his Master's feet. He realized that they had been emancipated from their cycle of birth and death.

On one occasion, Guru Angad* had received a set of clothes from his in-laws and Guru Angad happily wore his new attire. Shortly after, Guru Nanak asked him: 'Go and fetch grass!' Then Guru Angad* unhesitatingly left to complete the task and brought it from the paddy; however, his new clothes were soiled and laced with mud. On seeing the foul condition of Guru Angad's attire, Guru Nanak's mother got sullen and remonstrated to her son: 'You have inculcated him to follow your path and have strayed him from worldly tasks. He belongs to someone else and now he has been indoctrinated to follow your strange ways! He has come here after performing your task and his clothes are soiled with mud.' On hearing this, the Baba laughed and said: 'O Mother! This is not mud, it is sandalwood which is of both spiritual and material worlds.' The mother understood the hidden message and thereafter kept silent.

After a while, the Baba went to sleep. When it was time to eat, the maid went over to Guru Nanak and tried to wake him up. She saw the divine posture of the Guru and out of devotion, she decided to clean the Baba's feet by using her tongue. While performing this task, she envisioned that the Baba was standing in the sea. He was offering salvation to his devotees by pushing the ship of his followers out of the worldly sea. Soon after, Guru Nanak's mother also came over, and asked: 'Is Nanak awake?' The maid replied: 'Nanak is not here, mother! He is standing in the sea.' Surprised at what she heard, the mother got furious and struck the maid with her hands. The mother said: 'She too has started making jokes at me.' On hearing the commotion, the Baba woke up and his mother complained: 'O son! This maid has also commenced jesting at me. She says that 'Baba is standing in the sea.' In order to calm down his mother, the Baba said: 'O Mother! Don't get swayed by what this foolish maid says; she was hallucinating.' The maid had however received a divine vision of the Guru and after her short, delirious moment and with the grace of Guru Nanak joined the *congregation. Many others became Name-devoted followers of the Guru after hearing this narration.

## 54. Lehna becomes Angad

One day, according to the will of the Almighty, Gorakh Nath paid a visit at the abode of Guru Nanak and said: 'You have established a large congregation with many followers.' The Baba replied: 'Gorakh Nath! Out of these multitude of devotees, you will see with your own eyes who are my true followers.'

Shortly after Baba Ji came out of his dharamsala and his 'so called' followers started escorting him and were curious as to where the Guru would lead them to. While they were walking and to everyone's surprise the ground on which they were treading was miraculously covered with money. Many from the congregation, could not resist the urge to enrich themselves and started picking up the coins and forgot about the Baba.

There were some devotees who followed Guru Nanak and after walking a little bit further, saw that rupees were spread all round them. Many were overcome with the longing to gather the currency and started filling up their pockets while the Baba moved on.

The remaining few who still followed the Guru saw that the ground ahead was full of *mohurs.* They could not hold back their avarice and stayed back to accumulate as much as they could. Finally, only two disciples were left with the Guru and they proceeded with him.

As they went ahead, they found a pyre burning at a distance. Four lamps were lit on it and a dead person was lying there, covered with a sheet. The surrounding had a bad odor and was it was unbearable for the followers to breathe due to the foul smell. The Baba commanded his followers by saying: 'Is there anyone who would eat this corpse?' At that time, one of the devotees became nauseated and in sheer revulsion, turned his face on the other side and expectorated. Soon after, he left the place and came back home.

In the end, only one disciple remained at the spot and he was Guru Angad*. On receiving the orders from his Master, he obediently stayed steadfast and asked: 'On which side, my Lord, should I begin with?' Then instructions were delivered: 'Set your mouth towards the feet.' Guru Angad went over and as soon as he lifted the sheet and to his utter amazement, he saw that Guru Nanak was lying there.

Gorakh Nath exclaimed: 'Nanak! Your next Guru shall be the one who begets from your own self being.' Thereafter, Guru Nanak bestowed the name Guru Angad upon Lehna and after witnessing the conclusion of the episode, Gorakh Nath took leave.

As Baba came back to his place, his followers started repenting and thought that they could have received more had they stayed on and followed the Guru further. The ones who picked up the coins would say: 'Had we gone ahead, we would have received rupees.' The ones who accumulated the rupees said: 'Had we gone ahead, we could have piled up *mohurs.'*

The Baba then recited the following *Sabad* in Rag Sri Rag M:1:-

**Siri Rag Mehla 1.** *In account the man speaks the words, in account he partakes of the food. In account he walks along the way, in account he hears and sees. In account he draws the breath. Why should I go ask the literate?1. O Father! Deceitful is the splendour of worldly* *object. The (spiritually) blind man has forgotten God's name. He neither abides in peace in this world nor in the next.1. Pause. Life and death are for everything that is born. Death devours everything here. Where the Righteous Judge sits and explains the account, thither no one goes with the man. The weepers, one and all, tie bundles of straw.2. All say that the Lord is the greatest of the great. None calls Him less. No one has ascertained His worth. He becomes not great just by saying. Thou alone art the True Lord of mine and other being of numberless worlds.3. Nanak seeks the company of those who are of low caste among the lowly, nay rather the lowest of the low. Why should he (he has no desire to) rival the lofty? Where the poor are looked after, there does rain the look of Thy grace, O Lord! 4.3. (SGGS 15)*

## 55. Passing away of Makhdum Bahavadi

One day, as per the will of the Divine, a pious person by the name of Makhdum Bahavadi who was the Pir of Multan went along with his followers to offer Namaz on the auspicious day of *Eid*. Soon after, Makhdum Bahavadi felt sorrowful and tears filled his eyes and he started laminating. Seeing the melancholies mood of their master, the followers asked: 'Long live, O Pir! Why did you weep?' Then Makhdum Bahavadi said: 'O men of God! This is not worth telling.' The followers insisted: 'Be you live long, O Pir. Kindly tell us about it.' Then Makhdum Bahavadi said: 'O dear ones! No one shall maintain trust or faith from today; all shall become dishonest.' Then the followers said: 'Be you live long, O Pir! Be kind and tell us.' And then Makhdum Bahavadi said: 'O Friends! When a Hindu shall go to heaven, there shall be light all around there.

Many wise souls were present with the Pir and they could not keep their emotions in check and started asking: 'May you live forever, O Pir! As the liberated ones say that Hindus are not destined for heaven and you have also said so; therefore, how shall we know what you are saying is true now?' Then Makhdum Bahavadi said: 'If there is any literate and wise one amongst you, bring him over.' Then they presented an erudite person and Makhdum Bahavadi wrote one *Saloka :-*

**Whatever load hast we loaded, of what avail shall it be for us?**

From his mouth, he said that 'Nanak is the name of that Dervish and he lives in 1 Talwandi. Give this note to him when he asks for it.' Then the man departed for the destination. After reaching there, he sat at a distance of two *Kos* and said: 'If Nanak is true, he shall send for me.' Soon after, Baba sent for Bhasma, his devotee and instructed him: 'There is a man in the garden, and he has come from Multan. He is a disciple of Makhdum Bahavadi. Please bring him here.' The devotee went to the garden and brought the messenger in the presence of the Guru. The man came near and kissed Guru's feet. The Guru asked for the piece of paper and read it. Makhdum Bahavadi had written:-

**Whatever load hast we loaded, of what avail shall it be for us?**

The Baba wrote the Saloka above the original Saloka:-

**Whatever worked for shall be loaded, all are under order of His Will.**

**Radiant are faces of those, says Nanak, who go after earning the right. 1.**

The Baba wrote 'Liberated, Liberated' to Makhdum Bahavadi and said: 'You proceed on. I too shall come after forty days. Thereafter, the Sabad was recited, in Rag Sri Rag M:1:-

*Wealth, youth and flowers are guests only for four days. Like the leaves of water lily, they whither, fade (and finally) die away.1. Enjoy Lord's love, O dear one! So long as thou hast buoyant fresh youth. Few are thine days, thou hast grown weary and thy body vesture has grown old.1. Pause. My sportful friends have gone to sleep in the graveyard. I, double-minded, too shall depart and weep with feeble voice.2. Within thine ears, O my fair-coloured soul, why thou hearest not this fact? Thou shall go to the in-laws and cannot stay with thy parents for ever.3. O Nanak, know that she, who is asleep in her parents' home, is burgled in broad-day light. She is departing after having lost her bundle of merits and has tied one of demerits.4.24. (SGGS 23)*

The messenger came back to Multan after meeting Guru Nanak. Makhdum Bahavadi came out with his disciples to see his follower who handed the message to his master. Makhdum Bahavadi, on seeing the note, started bewailing.

Seeing the unusual behaviour of their Pir, the disciples asked: 'Why did you weep, Master?' Makhdum Bahavadi replied: 'O friends! I had written - if you go, I will come along with you. We shall go together to God's court.' Guru Nanak has replied by stating: 'you go; we shall come after forty days.' 'O friends! I am worried because for forty days I shall have to live in dark, all alone. O friends! I'm remorseful for those lonely forty days as I don't know how I shall spend them by myself? If he had come along with me, we would have departed quite comfortably in the divine light.' After saying these words, Makhdum Bahavadi breathed his last. Thereafter, the disciples felt sad and consoled each other and offered their prayers from the bottom of their heart to the departed soul.

# 56. Guruship to Sri Guru Angad Ji

One day Baba Ji came towards the bank of River Ravi. He placed five paise before Guru Angad Ji and offered him his obeisance by touching his feet. When others witnessed this event, they went back to Guru Nanak's family and word spread amongst the entire congregation that Guru Baba would be departing soon from their presence to merge with the divine.

Later on, Guru Angad stood with his hands folded in front of Guru Nanak and on seeing him in the form of a supplicant, the Baba expressed: 'Ask for something.' Guru Angad Ji said: 'O my Lord! If it pleases you, the congregation that has started to separate herewith, kindly bless it so that it remains intact as it has always been, since its inception.' Then a word came to Guru Angad that: 'By grace of you, the congregation is blessed.' Immediately, Guru Angad fell at Baba's feet. Following this, a *Sabad* was recited in Rag Majh Mehla 1:- 1

**Majh Mehla 5.** *Like warp and woof, the Lord is intertwined with His servant. The comfort-giver Lord cherishes His serf. I carry water, wave fan and grind grain for the (God's) attendant who has the longing and occupation of the Lord's service. The Lord has cut my noose and yoked me to His service. The order of the Lord is pleasing to His slave's mind. He does that what is pleasing to his Master. Within and without, the servant becomes supreme. Thou art the wise Master and knowest all ways. The Lord's serfs enjoy God's affection. What belongs to the Lord that belongs to His page. The page is distinguished in the association of his Lord. He, whom his Master clothes with the robe of honour, is not called to account again. To that servant, Nanak is a sacrifice. He is the pearl of the deep and infinite Lord. (SGGS 101-102)*

# 57. Baba's Passing Away

Guru Baba went over and sat under a tree. The tree had been dry for many years. As soon as Guru Nanak sat under it, the tree became green and started to flourish with new leaves and flowers. Soon after, Guru Angad came over and on seeing the Guru seated under the tree, he offered his respect and bowed at Baba's feet. Guru Nanak's mother was nearby and could not witness the final moments of her son's departure; she started wailing and weeping. Thereafter, a *Sabad* was recited. The assembled congregation, including close family members who felt somber and started to cry. Then the following *Sabad* in Rag Wadhans was recited:-

## Rag Wadhans Mehla 1.

*Blessed is the Creator, the True King, who has engaged the world in its tasks. When the time is over and the measure is full, this dear soul is caught and driven off. When the writ is received, the dear soul is driven off and all the brethren bewail. When mortal's days are at an end, the body and the swan soul are separated, O my mother. As is the writ and as are his former acts, so obtains he. Hail to the Creator, the True King, who has engaged the world in its task. Remember the Lord, O my brethren. All have to go this way. The false strife here is only for four (a few) days and then one assuredly proceeds onwards. For sure, one proceeds into the Yond like a guest. Why should then one indulge in ego? Repeat the Name of Him, by serving whom, thou shalt obtain peace in His court. In the next world, in no way, can man's command run. Everyone fares according to his acts. Meditate on the Lord, O my brethren, for all shall have to go this way. Whatever pleases the Omnipotent Lord that alone comes to pass. This world is an opportunity to earn His pleasure. The True Creator is pervading the ocean, the earth, the nether regions and the firmament. The True Creator is invisible and infinite. His limit cannot be determined. Fruitful is the advent of those, who, single-mindedly, contemplate over the Lord. The Adorner, by His command, demolishes, and having demolished, Himself constructs. Whatever pleases the All-powerful Lord that happens. This world is an opportunity to earn His pleasure. Says Nanak, O father, one is deemed to weep truly, if one weeps in the Lord's love. O father, the mortal bewails for the sake of worldly objects; therefore, all his bewailing is in vain. All the weeping is in vain. The world is forgetful of the Lord and weeps for wealth. Between good and evil, the mortal does not make any discrimination and wastes away this life in vain. All those who come here shall go. Hence false it is to act in pride. Says Nanak, O father, a man is considered to wail truly, if he wails in the Lord's love.4.1. (SGGS 578-579)*

The gathering started to chant *Alahnian* – the mournful dirges. While this was going on, the Baba was absorbed in his thoughts and reached an ecstatic state of mind. He received the divine order to set Rag Tukhari. Baba started to recite *Baramah*. It was night time and when the ambrosial hour set in, the moment for departure of the Guru had arrived:-

## Tukhari Chhant 1St Guru. Baramah – twelve months.

*Hear Thou O Lord! Each individual enjoys peace and suffers sorrow, as a result of the deeds done in the past. Whatever Thou givest, that is good. O God, creation is Thine. Of what account am I? My Lord, without Thee, I can live not even for a moment. Without my Beloved, I am miserable. I have no friend. It is by the Guru's grace, that I drink Nectar. The Formless Lord is contained in His creation. The act of obeying the Lord is the best of all the acts. O Nanak, Thy bride is beholding Thy way. Hear Thou, O Omnipresent spirit!1. The sparrow-hawk cries 'Beloved' and the cuckoo sings the lays. The bride enjoys all the pleasures and merges in the Being of her Love. When she becomes pleasing to her Lord God, then merges she in His Being. She is the happy bride. Establishing the nine houses and a royal mansion above them, God, the Enemy of ego, abides in that mansion of His. All art Thine, Thou art my Beloved. Night and day, make I merry in Thine love. Nanak, the sparrow-hawk of the mind cries 'Spouse, my Spouse' and the cuckoo of the tongue is embellished with the Name.2. Hear Thou, O God, my Beloved, drenched am I in Thine love. With my soul and body repeat and utter I Thy Name. Thee, I forget not even for a moment. How can I forget Thee even for an instant? I live by singing Thy praise, O Lord. A sacrifice unto Thee, am I. No one belongs to me. To whom belong I? Without my Lord, I can live not. I have grasped the refuge of God's feet and abide there, and my body has become immaculate. Nanak, I have obtained deep vision and peace and with the Guru's word my soul is consoled.3. It rains a torrent of elixir. Delightful are its drops. When Guru, the friend, meets in the natural way, then love with the Lord is established. The Lord God comes into the body-temple when it pleases Him and the bride rising up utters His praise. In every home, the Spouse enjoys the chaste brides. Why hast the Spouse forgotten me? The lowering clouds have over-spread the sky. It rains pleasantly and the Lord's love is pleasing to my soul and body. Nanak, when the ambrosial Gurbani rains, the Lord graciously comes into my home.4. In Chet agreeable is the spring and beautiful the bumble-bee. The forests are flowering in front of my door. May my Love return home! How can the bride obtain peace, when her Spouse comes not home? With the distress of separation, her body is wasting away. The beauteous cuckoo sings on the mango-tree. How can I bear the pain of my mind? The black-bee is flitting on the blossoming bough. How can I survive? I am dying, O Mother. Nanak, in Chet peace is easily obtained, if the wife obtains God as her Spouse in her home.5. Pleasant is Baisakh, when the tree-bough adorns itself anew. The bride is anxious to see God at her door. "Come, my Love, come. Take Thou pity on me". Come home, O my Beloved! Ferry me across the difficult world-ocean. Without Thee, I am not worth even a shell. Who can appraise my worth, if I please Thee? I see Thee and show Thee to others, O my Love. O Lord, I know Thee not afar. I believe Thee to be within me, and realize I Thine presence. Nanak, whosoever obtains the Lord in Baisakh, his soul is satiated with Name's meditation.6. Sublime is the month of Jeth. Why should I forget my Beloved? The earth burns like a furnace. The bride prays to her Lord. The bride makes supplication and utters His praise. Singing the Lord's praise, I become pleasing to Him. The Detached Lord abides in the true mansion. If He permits me to go to Him, then will I go to him. Unhonoured and powerless is the bride. How can she obtain peace without her Lord? In Jeth, O Nanak, she who knows her Lord, becomes like Him and grasping virtue through His grace, she meets with Him.7. Good is the month of Asad, when the sun blazes in the sky. The earth suffers sorrow and is parched and heated like fire. The heat dries up moisture and men die in anxiety. Even then the sun wearies not in his task. The sun's chariot moves on, the wife looks for the shade and the grass-hoppers chirp in the forest. She, who departs, tying the bundle of sins, suffers hereafter and she, who remembers the True Lord, obtains peace. Nanak, my death and life are with the Lord, to whom I have surrendered this soul of mine.8. In Sawan, be thou happy, O my soul. The season has come when the clouds rain. I love my Spouse with my soul and body, but my Darling has gone abroad. My Beloved comes not home. I am dying with the sorrow of separation. The flash of lighening terrifies me. Lonely is my couch, and I am greatly grieved. I am dying of pain, O my mother. Say, without God, how can sleep and appetite come to me? The raiments afford my body no comfort. Nanak, she alone is the chaste bride who merges in the being of her Beloved Spouse.9. In Bhadon, the bride in the bloom of youth strays in doubt, but she afterwards regrets. The ponds and meadows are filled with water. It is the rainy season, the time of merry-making. It rains during the dark night. How can the young bride have peace? The frogs and peacocks shriek. 'Beloved, beloved' cries the pied-cuckoo and the snakes go about biting. The mosquitoes sting and the pools are filled to the brim. Without her Lord, how can the wife obtain comfort? I will ask my Guru and walk accordingly. Whithersoever my Lord is, thither shall I go.10. In Asu, come, O my Beloved. Thy wife is repining herself to death. If the Lord makes her meet, than alone can she meet with Him, but the bride is ruined by the love of another. When the bride is disfigured by falsehood, then the Spouse forsakes her. Then bloom the reed and tamarisk diocia. Summer is left behind and the winter season lies ahead. Seeing this play, my mind wavers. All over the ten sides of the boughs are green and verdant. That which slowly ripens, is sweet. Meet Thou me, O my Love in Assu. The True Guru has become my mediator.11. In Katak, what pleases the Lord is recorded in the mortal's destiny. The lamp, which is lit by quintessence, that easily burns. Love is the oil of the lamp that unites the bride with her Groom. The bride is in bliss and bloom. She, whom sin kills, becomes not fruitful at her death. When killed by virtue, then dies she easily. They, whom Thou, O Lord, blesseth with Thy Name and devotional service, sit in their own home. Even then their hope rests on Thee. Says Nanak, "O Lord, open the shutters of Thy door and meet me. A moment, now, is like six months to me,"12. Good is the month of Maghar for those, who merge in the Lord's Being, by singing His praise. The virtuous wife utters the Lord's praise. My ever-stable Love is pleasing to me. Moveless, Wise and Omniscient is my Creator-Lord, but the whole world is movable. They, who possess the virtue of gnosis and meditation, merge in the Lord's Being. They are pleasing to the Lord and the Lord is pleasing to them. The songs, music and the poems of poets have I heard, but it is through the Lord's Name that sorrow flees. Nanak, only that bride is dear unto her Groom, who in His presence, performs the hearty service of her Beloved.13. In Poh, the snow falls and the sap of the forest and grass dries up. O Lord, why comest Thou not? Thou abidest within my soul, body and mouth. God, the Life of the world, is permeating my mind and body. Through the Guru's word, enjoy I His love. The Lord's Light is contained in the egg-born, the foetus-born, the sweat-born and all the hearts. O Lord of compassion, the Beneficent One! Bless me with Thy vision and grant me understanding, that I may obtain salvation. Nanak, with love and pleasure, God, the*

*Enjoyer, enjoys the bride, who bears Him love and affection.14. In the month of Magh, I become immaculate by realizing that the place of pilgrimage is within me. I have easily met my Friend, by enshrining His virtues and by merging in His Being. Hear thou me, O my darling and beauteous Lord. Thy merits I have enshrined in my mind. If it pleases Thee, I shall bathe in Thy tank. The Ganges, the Jamuna, the confluence of three streams, seven oceans, charity, alms and worship are contained in the Lord's Name. I realize that the One Lord is pervading in every age. Nanak, in Magh, the ablution at the sixtyeight holies is contained in the meditation of the Supreme elixir of the Lord's Name.15. In Phagan, the soul of those, to whom Lord's love is pleasing, is in bloom. She, who effaces her self-conceit, night and day, abides in spiritual bliss. When it pleases Him, efface I the worldly love from my mind and the Lord mercifully comes to my home. Though I may wear many garbs, yet without Love, I shall find not a place in His mansion. When my Beloved so wished, I decorated myself with garlands, strings of pearls, perfumes and raiments of silk. Nanak, the Guru has united me with God and I, the bride, have obtained my Groom in my very home.16. The two and ten (twelve) months, the seasons, the lunar days, the week days, the hours, the minutes and moments are all sublime, when the True Lord comes and naturally meets me. The sweet Master has met me and mine affairs are arranged. The Creator Lord knows all the ways. I am dear unto Him, who has embellished me. I have met Him and enjoyed His love. The couch of my home becomes beauteous, when my Beloved enjoys me. By the Guru's grace, the destiny of my forehead is awakened. Nanak, day and night, my Beloved enjoys me and obtaining God as my Spouse my married life has become eternal.17. 1. (SGGS 1107-1110*

The Guru recited the *Sabad* which reached Guru Angad in the composition of *pothi* (the written form) and verbal form. Seeing their father on the verge of departing this world, his sons came over and asked him: 'What shall become of us?' The Guru spoke the word: 'O sons! Everyone, even the lowest of the low finds grace and security in the abode of Guru. You shall have plenty of food and clothing. As you shall remember the Guru, your life will lead you towards a righteous path.'

Soon after, the devotees, including both: Hindus and Muslims started arguing. The Muslims said: 'We shall bury him' and the Hindus started saying: 'We shall cremate him'. The Baba intervened and appeased his followers by saying: 'Please keep flowers on both sides of my body. On the right, Hindus will place their flowers and on the left Muslims will lay down their flowers. By morning if the flowers of Hindus appear fresh, then I may be cremated and if the flowers of Muslims appear fresh, then I may be buried.' The Baba asked his congregation to: 'Recite *Kirtan*'. Obeying the Master's command, the disciples started chanting the *Kirtan* (singing of devotional songs) in Rag Gauri Purbi Mehla 1.

### *Sohila Rag Gauri Deepki Mehla 1;*

*There is but one God. By the True Guru's grace, He is obtained.*

*The house in which the Creator is meditated upon and His praises are repeated, in that house sing the songs of praise and remember the Maker.1. Do thou sing the songs of praise of the Fearless Lord. I am a sacrifice unto the song of joy by which eternal solace is procured.1. Pause. Ever and ever, the Lord watches over His beings and the Giver is beholding one and all. No price can be put on thine gifts. How can, then, that Giver's (Thy) estimation be had?2. The year and the day of wedding (recorded) is fixed. Meet together my mates and pour oil at the door. Give me your blessings, O Friends, that I may attain union with my Master.3. This summon is sent to every house and such calls do daily come. Meditate on the Summoner, O Nanak, that day is approaching near.4.1. (SGGS 12-13)*

*Rag Asa Mehla 1. There are six systems, six their teachers and six their doctrines. But the teacher of teachers is but one Lord, thou He has various vestures.1. O father, the house (system) where-in the praises of the Creator are uttered, follow that system. In it rests thy greatness.1. Pause. As seconds, minutes, hours, quarters of a day, lunar days, week days, months and several seasons spring from the lone sun, so many forms originate from the Creator, O Nanak! 2.2.*

Dhanasari Rag was set and *aarti* was performed. Guru's *Sabad* was sung and Salok recited:-

*Air is the Guru, water the Father, the earth the great Mother, and day and night the two female and male nurses, in whose lap the entire world plays. The merits and demerits shall be read in the presence of Righteous Judge. According to their respective deeds, some shall be near and some distant (from the Lord). Who have pondered on the Name, and have departed after putting in toil, O Nanak, their faces shall be bright and many shall be emancipated along with them. (SGGS 8)*

As the *Saloka* were being recited, Baba went to sleep by placing a sheet of cloth over himself and covered his entire body. The congregation offered obeisance to the Baba. Afterwards, they lifted the sheet and to their surprise, there was nothing beneath it. The flowers on both sides were fresh. The Hindus took their side of the flowers and the Muslims theirs. Everyone assembled at the congregation and repeated the Lord's Name.

Everyone say *Waheguru*! Samvat 1595 dated Assu Sudi 10. Baba Nanak passed away at Kartarpur. All assembled recited: Waheguru1 Waheguru! Waheguru1 Waheguru! Waheguru! Waheguru!

This concludes the *Sakhi*. Everyone may be pardoned. Only Baba is unforgettable and ever reminiscing. Everyone devotionally say: 1Waheguru Ji Ki Fateh! All reliance upon You! 1.1.

***Do good deeds and the Lord shall always bless you. Anyone that appears on this earth shall perish one day. Neither a billionaire, nor his money nor his wealth, however abundant, shall stay on.***

### -Concluded-

# APPENDIX 1

## (From Sakhi 29)

*By grace of the True Guru. Religious practice of the Waheguru. Unison of four letters. It happened in forty Yugas. 40. Toiled sitting for forty Yugas. 41. The step moved forward. One crore seventy two lakh twenty eight thousand. 17228000. Infinite Yuga remained infinite in these Yugas. In tranquil state, it contemplated the awful wonder. Say, O Nanak, the saga of the Yuga Infinite. Contemplating His glory, all miseries vanished. 1. One crore sixty eight lakh forty eight thousand. 16848000. Rare ones exalted wonder of the Yuga. In tranquil state, all repeated the word. Say, O Nanak, the saga of the rare Yuga. Contemplating His glory, all miseries vanished. 2.*

(As such, after the 40 Yugas, this text is at the end of Yugawali) –

*What and where shall we relate Nanak's merits.*

*No god or human know the saga of this sect; Jugawali writing completed. Say all Waheguru. (Further, the text in the Sakhi ahead is as such):- By grace of the True Guru. Then Baba felt pleased. Jhanda badhi was seen off to Bisiar country. The diocese of Jhanda Badhi is there in the Bisiar country. Kalyuga has prevailed for 4735 \*years; Kalyuga has sustained for four lakh twenty seven thousand two hundred and sixty five years. 4, 27, 265. Saint wrote the saga of forty Yugas. Hard toil of Waheguru. Further all grace of Waheguru. Total state of tranquility 13, 74, 32, 000. Total state of continence 9, 79, 14, 000. Total state of harmony 6, 21, 30, 000. Total state of pastness 28, 22, 80, 000. Total of the Satjuga 17, 28, 000. Total of Treta juga 12, 96, 000. Total of Duapar Juga 8, 64, 000. Total of the Kaljuga 4, 32, 000. Total of the Four Jugas 43, 20, 000. Total of Jugawali. Practice of the tranquil state of Jhanda Badhi. Practice of continence. Practice of the past state. Practice of the Satjuga. Practice of the Treta Juga. Practice of Duapar Juga. Practice of Kal Juga. Waheguru became gracious unto the towns of six river banks of Bisiar country ...*

---

(1) *This writing reveals that **Jugawali** was written after meeting Guru Angad Dev Ji. But when the Sakhi-writer says that Jugawali concluded', Guru Angad Dev Ji had not met then as yet, The reference of Jugawali connotes to one sect of Yogis and, as such, it appears to be the writing of some other book. At the end, it is clear that some Saint wrote this jugawali afterwards. It is not Guru's creation.*

- *From this detail, the Samvat of writing this Janam Sakhi becomes clear. The technique that Sardar Karm Singh Historian has given is as such: That that time Kalyuga had passed for 4735 years. Now in Bikrami 1983, Kalyug has passed for 5026 years.*

*No. of years passed= 5026*

No, of years passed then= 4735

---

Remainder = 0291.

It means that 291 years have passed when the Janam Sakhi was written; since the author of the Sakhi, after concluding Jugawali, writes on his behalf that Kalyug has passed for 4735 years.

So the era at present is 1983.

Subtracting 0291out of it, it comes to be 1692. As such, 291 years back, it was Samvat 1692. This is Samvat Bikrami 1692 that comes to be the year of writing the Sakhi. This is the period of Sixth Guru as 1701 Bikrami is the era of passing away of the sixth Guru.

# APPENDIX 2.

**(From Sakhi 36)**

# APPENDIX 3.

**(From Sakhi 47)**

Soul Exalted in the Unconscious state, is said all to be unconscious.

In the state of Soul Exalted, no pleasure or pain is realized.

In the state of Soul Exalted, no hope or doubt takes place.

In the state of Soul Exalted, np colour or creed appears.

In the state of Soul Exalted, no katha, kirtan or Bani is there.

In the state of Soul Exalted, one is centered in the unconscious.

In the state of Soul Exalted, one knows not one's own self.

The mind, says Nanak, unifies with state of the Exalted Soul.

In the state of Soul Exalted, no mother or father is any.

In the state of Soul Exalted, no worldly sense or sanity is there.

In the state of Soul Exalted, no mammon or affection is there.

In the state of Soul Exalted, the physique is never unconscious.

In the state of Soul Exalted, one thinks not of knowledge or intent.

In the state of Soul Exalted, one thinks not of freedom or paradise.

In the state of Soul Exalted, no sort of love or dedication is there.

Unto a state of Exalted Soul, says Nanak, they only comply with.

**(In total are 21 steps).**

---

# APPENDIX 4.

## No 1

*Salok. Killing of desire provides grace and one remains prime among the Five comrades. Whoever realses the secret of the Five, he only is the creator and god too. He who relates about the Inaccessible Vedas brings home the nine planets (sources of treasure) together. Seven to twenty-seven and fourteen to four stand before Him at the door. Eight and twenty-eight and twelve and twenty stand before and put forth the gospels. Exalted vision is ever of the jeweler and he only, says Nanak, is truly the detached one.1.4. He only is disenchanted who lives ever detached and resides among trees under the sky. Day and night, he practices Yoga and never*

*ever touches or comes near another. One who lets not let duality, doubt or filth of wickedness at heart, says Nanak, he only is truly detached being. Taking the sword of knowledge, he struggles he struggles with the mind and understands the dismal state of the five evils. He makes a knot of the mental conscience and worships at the three hundred and sixty pilgrimages. He who erases the filth of mind, he only, says Nanak, is truly detached one. Within the body are sixty eight points, most arduous point has the tiresome path. The True Guru revealed such a path and wandering about the ten directions one comes home calm and quiet. Some rare one unknots the secret of sixty-eight pilgrimages ad he ony, says Nanak, is truly the detached being. How merciful is he to roam about the sky and realizes, day and night, ever the month of Sawan(rainy season). Whoever is really the brave controls water, wind and fire. Whoever milked (subdued) the sky's cow, he only bids to be truly detached. At first, he looks towards the East and then treads towards the South. When he turns towards the Westfrom South, he comprehends about all places of merchandise. From the West, he goes up to Sumeir and returns after having a perambulation There at the top of seven sea-points lies lotus-seat of the lord and there lies the seat of the almighty. He who strings rosary of diamonds and rubies, says Nanak, he only is truly the detached one.*

## No. 2.

*Salok. Devotee of the Guru and celibate ever of the organ; liberated at heart and truthful in speech and with a graceful vision, he looks at the alms and whosoever bowe to is bowed truly. He who succeeds at the Word spoken, says Nanak, he only is true Yogi. Indulges not in physical pranksand visits not any show of sport; takes not part in gambling and plays no dice. He minds not any good or bad and wears the Guru-given dress ever. He visits not another\s house to have a discourse. Such is the Satguru-prone binding. Listen, O son! Guru's advice! He only is truly Yogi. He soars his mind towards the sky and sustains the string tied every day and night. On getting satisfied, he returns home. As such, a Yogi practices Yoga, and feeling no glee or sadness on going. Remains ever in control and nothing ejects out while sleeping, says Nanak, he only is truly Yogi. He swims anti-current to have onus-flow and remains immersed ever, day and night, in the Word. Reverse he turns the lotus and wind, and thus he evades coming and going. He keeps restricted the mental flow and maintains relation with the flow of the river. Within his control he keeps the agent as he only, says Nanak, is truly a Yogi.*

## No. 3.

*Salok.* In the posture of a saint, one ought to remain individual and keep the five elements well-restricted. One must have little sleep and scant sustenance. Be ever thoughtful in a saint's body; meditation, penance and check all the senses to have taste of. So are, says Nanak, the traits of Yoga. As he speaks be knower of all and, day and night, remain focused in the void. Have ever the link in the sublime void and, by grace of the Lord, never die. Perform, as such, Guru's service bound unto all the gods. Let the tongue not savour several tastes as such are, says Nanak, the traits of Yoga. Shed away wrath, desire and greed and burn the fire of five elements within. Remain ever, day and night, bearing the bow and the poise originates and all evils vanish. A saint is to be obliged and a thief be bound and repeat no other charm but of the Guru's Name. Superb and serene are the traits of their existence and so, says Nanak, are the traits of Yoga. One remains ever scrupulous with the five senses and through mouth one savours not the unknown. Well-read is he of the numberless billions of scriptures and keeps awareness of the horizons unknown. Irrigating the Netherlands he fills the sky-high pools. Going at Tribeni - the confluence three rivers, he takes a dip to bathe and adheres to the fove, seven nine bindings as these are, says Nanak, traits of Yoga. Going towards the East, he comes towards the West and unifies the sun and moon together. He realizes the distance between different places and then realizes the arduous shore. He visits the nine continents towards East, West, North and South as those are, says Nanak, traits of Yoga. Be this body a bowl and the conscience be milk. In that, we put the truth dissolving intently. Through effort and skill may realize the poise as tactless spending goes all waste. Knowledge is the churner and Name the cord, and by these means we remember and repeat the Name. By churning and churning, we cull out the butter as such are the traits, says Nanak, of a Jogi.

## No. 4.

*Disenchanted is he who surrenders in absolute and bows down all the might before the Lord. He exercises all powers of the Lord and bears the unbearable impulses of the unknowable through senses. Such a medication he may take unknowingly by taking of which all ills may vanish. He who relinquishes wrath, greed and ego, say Nanak, he is the disenchanted in the house of a worshipper. Realizing in mind the Word of Satguru, the wicked mental state departs as, says Nanak, he is in real the disenchanted being. Disenchanted is he who bears contentment and reverses the wind to remain calm and quiet. He captures the five evils as the disenchanted one goes up self-intentioned. Renouncing all the known, he sticks his senses to the One Being only as He only, says Nanak, is the Disenchanted Being. Disenchanted being is he who undergoes non-attachment and remembers the Lord through every breath. In the tranquil state, he remembers and repeats as that disenchanted one is real knower of the body elements. With sleep relinquished, one gets up in the void as truly he is, says Nanak, a disenchanted being. Disenchanted is he who annihilates semen and achieves, by Guru's grace, the Universe. In that knowledge of the void, he remains indivisible and keeps all the nine doors closed. In the tenth, he experiences the mystic music latent under the earth. As the tenth originates, it gets never vanished as there lies the abode of the Lord Supreme. There one realizes the secret of Lord Supreme as the disenchanted being pierces through time. Anyone who in this way goes through non-attachment, says Nanak, true taste of the Being. Disenchanted is he who remains liberated recluse and keeps his mind ever intoxicated by delving through twelve inlets. Sky is pool appearing with stringless tunes as the lightening brightens through clear radiance. Elixir, as such, rains and the saints go drenched. The individual too, as such, is the disenchanted being, says Nanak, by grace of the Guru's charm.*

# APPENDIX 5.

## (From Sakhi 51)

*With Alaf, initiate remembrance of God and forget negligence from the mind. Cursed is the living in this world if breath is heaved without the Name.1. With, Bey, shed away duality, and hold the step in faith. Walk lowly bowing to all and speak not evil to any.2. With Tey, make a solemn promise for a patient heart that lest you may repent. The body departs and the mouth is entombed, where shall you whine then? 3. With Sey, offer praise (of the Lord) in abundance and take not a single breath but that. While getting sold shop to shop, shall not get valued a pie even again.*

**-End-**

# BACK REFERENCE-NOTES.

## Sakhi 2.

- Sri Guru Nanak Dev Ji, while reading the 'patti' of Pandha, himself wrote this 'patti' alluded to spiritual meanings.

## Sakhi 3.

1. In the afore-said Sakhis, marriage is said to have taken place at Sultanpur. But Bhai Mani Singh Ji has said the marriage to have taken place here itself.

## Sakhi 7.

1. The Saloka is of Guru Two. Some copier has by mistake put it as Guru First.

## Sakhi 9.

1. The material that one gets besides the salary is termed as 'aloofa'.

## Sakhi 15.

1. A different reading is 'Ibrahim Beg'.

## Sakhi 16.

1. Wooden foot-wear with no support.

## Sakhi 18.

- The word pertains to mistake of the copier.

## Sakhi 19.

1. Difference of reading is *'dere'* instead of *'tande'*.

2. Instead of *'chupata raho'* the reading difference is *'char pehar'*.

3. In SGGS, the word *'pehre'* comes after *'Mehla 1'*.

# Sakhi 22.

1. We have given the pure version of the *sabad* as it is in SGGS.

2. This *sabad* is of the Fifth Guru. It is mistake of the copier that it is given 'Mehla 1' in the *pothi*.

# Sakhi 28.

• The dignitary appears to be Seikh Farid Sani, whose name comes as Seikh Brahm in Sakhis. Going ahead, the Sakhi 32 has taken place with this Seikh Brahm. If both the Sakhis have taken place with the same one Farid, the writer has mistakenly put gap in the two Sakhis. Both should have been in one sequence. Or the second Sakhi was to observe the effect of the first one as both the Sakhis in *Bhai Mani Singh Ji di Sakhi* have been told with the same Seikh Brahm, and it has been written before the second meeting:- 'Baba said: 'Mardana! We are to go to Pattan as we had instructed Seikh Brahm and it is to be seen whether he remembers that instruction or has forgotten'. This is probable too that some other Faqir in Asa Desh be having the same epithet and he be conversant with the Bani of first Farid. Taking it so as the writer of this 'Janam Sakhi' had no information about the erstwhile living of Seikh Farid will construe to be a lapse since, in Sakhi 32, he clearly writes that 'Seikh Farid was Pir of Pattan and his successor was Seikh Brahm'. So the writer had correct information that Farid the First had expired and Seikh Birahm (Farid Sani) was holding his seat. So here at no reference can be made to Seikh Farid the First.

3. This Salok is that of the fifth Guru. It is an err on the writer's part.

4. Further from here is 'Jugawali' As a specimen, it is given in Appendix 1. This Jugawali is not in SGGS, and neither is it Gurbani.

# Sakhi 31.

1. To say 'Kalu' only here in singular appears lack of respect. But this is lapse on the writer's part because when Kalu came there to see Guru Ji sitting at the same place, then Guru Ji got up to offer obeisance to his father, and that is written in the Sakhi. As such, if he was so respectful to his father in actual, how could he be different in saying?

2. Going a little further, Mother asks Mardana to help her meet Nanak. Then Mardana offers no reply and keeps mum. It implies that Mardana still kept silence and gave no reply in response. This shrewdness is of some copier, and it is not in the writing of the original writer.

# Sakhi 32.

1. This Salok pertains to Guru 3 in SGGS in Rag Gujri. Giving it here is a lapse on the writer's part.

2. It appears that Guru Ji's reply is in the next Salok. But the author or the writer has written the extra Salok from his oral memory. The two lines are not from SGGS.

3. In Asa di Vaar, this Salok of Guru 2 has been kept by the fifth Guru while compiling the Vaar. When the discourse with Seikh Brahm was held, the Salok was not there at that time.

# Sakhi 33.

1. This *sabad* is of Guru Fourth. Some writer at the time of copying has written it out of memory. Had he written it taking as Gurbani, he would have realized it of Mehla 4. Whatever the sabads on lamentation of the Faqir, have been said, is as per the time and this *sabad* is superfluous, and that appears to have been added by some previous writer.

## Sakhi 34.

1. The mendicants in the poem of Nazeer are the changed forms of this song.

## Sakhi 35.

1. Killing at Saedpur jail was not because of Guru Ji's wrath. In the sabad, Guru Ji is simply conveying the revelation come from the Lord. Himself, he is unattached and is reviling Babar's action. It is clear that he never cursed in any way. Alleging 'wrath' is omission on the writer's part.

2. The author has made this sermon from his own self.

3. This *sabad* is by Guru Fourth. It has come here by lapse of the author himself or because of copier. The sabad that Guru Ji recited at that time is in page 360 of SGGS.

4. This *sabad* is by the Fifth Guru. The lapse pertains to the author or the writer.

5. Guru Ji was telling the general behavior of the world. Whatever is omission, he is cutting a joke at it. He is not telling it as the divine law.

6. The reference has long story. Then he went and joined the army. Babar, the Emperor, was a monk. He ruled during the day and would at night put chains at feet and meditated with head upside down. Getting up at last part of night, he used to meditate a lot. As there came the morning, he would get up and offer *Namaz*. At the third watch, he read Quran and thereafter take hemp. As Baba entered the forces, he started singing hymns. The prisoners also got aside. On looking at the prisoners, Baba felt much humble and meek. Then baba said: 'Mardana1 Play the *rabab*. Then Baba recited the *sabad* in Rag Asa.

As Babar the Emperor listened to this song, he said: 'O Friends! Bring this faqir'. Then the men went and brought Baba to be present. Then Babar said: 'O revered Faqir! Please repeat the *sabad* you have just recited'. Then Baba recited the *sabad* again. Then Babar acquired realization. Then Babar said: 'O Friends! This Faqir is learned one'. Then he opened the smack of hemp, placed it before the Baba and said: 'O Faqir! Do have hemp'. Then Baba said: 'O Emperor! I have taken hemp. I have taken such hemp as it is never diffused'. Then Babar said: 'What is that drug the intoxication of which does never subside?

Then Baba said: 'Mardana! Play the *rabab*. Then Baba recited the *sabad* in Rag Tilang: (SGGS 360)

*O Lord, Thy fear is my hemp and my mind is the leather pouch. I have become an intox-icated hermit. My hands are the begging bowl and I crave for Thine vision, O God. Day by day, beg I at Thy door.1. For Thy sight, I make a mumper's call. Bless Thou me, Thine door's beggar, with alms, O Lord.1. Pause. Saffron, flowers, deer's musk and gold embel-lish all, the bodies. Like Chandan, such is the quality of Lord's slaves that they render fragrant one and all.2. No one calls clarified butter and silk polluted. Such is the saint, be he of high or low caste. They who make obeisance unto Thy Name and remain absorbed in Thy love, O Nanak, I beg at their door for alms.3.1.2. (SGGS 721)*

When Baba recited this *sabad*, Emperor Babar felt much happy, and said: 'O Respected Faqir! Go with me'. Then Baba said: 'O Emperor! I shall live with you for one day'. Babar then said again: 'You kindly live for three days'. Then Baba said: 'I shall live'. But Baba lamented much on looking at the prisoners. Then Baba said: 'O Mardana! Play the *rabab*. Mardana played the *rabab* and Baba recited the *sabad* in Raga Asa. (No *sabad* is given here. But it appears to be the same *sabad* . Thereat Baba came to himself. Baba kept lying when Babar came and stood there. Babar said: 'What happened to the Faqir?' People said: 'O Master! He is a dervish. He has come to the state on seeing the Lord's wrath'. Then Babar said: O Friends! Join hands unto the Lord to make this *Faqir* stand up'. Then Baba got up. With getting up of Baba, there was such a dazzling light as if many thousands of suns had risen. Then Babar offered greetings, and said: 'You be benevolent, Master'. Then Baba said: 'O Emperor! If you ask for benevolence, then set free all the prisoners'. Then Babar said: 'I have a request, Master. I may say if allowed.' Then Baba said: 'Do say.' Babar said: 'If you give me one word, I release them all.' Baba said: 'Ask for something.' Then Babar said: 'O Master! I ask for this only that my kingship may continue from one to the next successor.' Then Baba said: 'Your kingship shall last long.' Then Babar offered greetings. The total prisoners were set free. Then Baba felt much pleased. Then Baba Nanak departed from Babar, and went further from there. Say all 'Waheguru'!

7.  This too is not Gurbani. In Majh Ki Vaar in SGGS, it is different.

8.  These lines are not composed by Mian Mitha. The question itself is composed by Guru Ji himself in the *sabad*. Guru Ji, generally, used to write question-answers composed by himself after the discourse, as is evident from the Sidh Gost.

9.  This *sabad* is composition of Guru Fifth. In actual book, the *sabad* is given of Mehla 1. This is an error on the part of the writer. At the time of some copying, the copier wrote this *sabad* in detail from his learning by heart without clarifying that the *sabad* is not if Guru First.

10. Ahead of this is *Hazarnama*. See Appendix 2 at the end. Not being in SGGS, it is not Gurbani.

## Sakhi 39.

•   This *sabad* is by the Fifth Guru. Writing of First Guru is a mistake.

## Sakhi 41.

1.  By writing *Beid,* the writer does not mean it to be Ved, but some other scripture.

## Sakhi 42.

1.  This Salok is by Guru 2. It is wrong on the writer's part.

2.  This Salok is at the end of *Japuji* too. A similar Salok with some difference is in Vaar Majh M: 2 also. A similar Salok with some differences is in Rag Maru M:1(1025) .

## Sakhi 44.

1.  This Salok is by the Fifth Guru. Writing of Mehla 1 is wrong on the writer's part.

## Sakhi 45.

1.  The reference appears to refer to successor of Farid, Seikh Ibrahim, whom Guru Ji had met twice before and offered sermon to him.

## Sakhi 46.

1.  Gorakh Nath did not know that Guru Nanak Dev ji had already told about his Guru: (SGGS 599). Gorakh Nath perhaps wanted to say that he should not bow before anyone but the one whom you complete yourself; and it can be a cue towards Guru Angad Dev Ji. Guru Nanak Dev Ji has himself told about not bowing before anyone: meant to say that 'but for the Supreme Lord *Waheguru*, none else appears to sit spreading the rug before me'.

## Sakhi 47.

1.  This narration refers to test. The Raja had tested the Guru at first by sending amorous females. That was 'Guru's test'. Now Guru Ji did the 'Sikh test'. Such tests connote to sacrifice of the son of Mordhuj among Hindus and that of the sonof Ibrahim among Muslims. Should the asking of sacrifice appear objectionable, the competence to make the son alive makes it clear. If the making of reliving be doubted, the asking of sacrifice too needs to be doubted since both the versions at the same place are of the same pen. Such imagination is of the writer himself. In reference to Guru Ji's nature, such strict tests make no congruence with Bani of the Guru.

2.  Ahead of this is the Bani given in Appendix 3. It is not in SGGS, and its name is 'Pran Sangli'. In this Bani, the word *unman* – aunmin – sublimity of soul. Such a state of mind has explicitly been described. It amounts to the rise of the mental state or conscience above the state of delight or dismay and remain ever in realization of aggrandizement of the faith and balance of inner soul.

3.  The reference pertains to realize knowledge about physical state. But the next line appears to tell about some book. It refers to some mistake on the writer's part. The *pothi* refers to *Pran Sangli* which was written there and left there. It was given to Raja Shiv Nabh and he was asked to send it to Hindustan when someone comes from there. So the reference caters to different sense.

## Sakhi 49.

1. Once it came to be known in Kashmir that Brahm Das was a resident of the town Beej Bihara, and he came in contact with Guru Ji at the spring Martand. Since then, it is called 'Mattan Sahib'. A mound was there in middle of the spring, whereat they sat and had the discourse. The village people became devotees of the Guru. The mound is in ruin state now. During the time of Maharaja Ranjit Singh, six volumes of Guru Granth Sahib were made to manifest round the pool there in the *Dharamsala*. That *Dharamsala* is no more these days. But a new *Dharamsala* has been built at a little distance, and the Granth manifestation is held there. About a mile away, the temple of Martand is there, though in ruinous state, at Karewa Pabbi

2. Most likely, the hint is towards the demolished Martand temple at Karewa, where Brahm Das had a vision of Maya – mammon - in female form who had warned him. One arch of the temple is standing as yet, rest all the stones have fallen; those have been demolished by idol-breakers.

## Sakhi 50.

1. Ahead of Martand, '*Amarnath*' is the temple of Shiva Ji, but it is not very far. From the mountain '*Swalakh*', the hint appears to be *Kailash*. Near to it are the mountains from where gold is found. 'Sumeir' appears to refer to those mountains. 'Maan Sarovar' too is near to 'Kailash'. This is a great pilgrimage center of Bodhis and Hindus. Yogis or Sidhas came to visit the place and met SatGuru Ji appears to have met them here. 'Kailash' is said to be the place of Shiva.

2. 'Maha Deo' is the name of some Yogi, not to confuse with Shiva. Going ahead, Mahadeo speaks and tell his name as 'Ishar'. 'Ishar' is used for 'Mahadeo' also.

3. Reference is to bring the vessel filled from 'Maan Sarovar'.

   - Question and answers to these *Salokas* are within them. But the author of the Sakhi has taken answers from the Ratan Mala also. See Appendix 4.

   - A sect of Yogis i.e. *Jainis* and *Bodhis* etc.

   - Bhai Gurdas Ji has given detail of this discourse in Vaar First.

*Baba saw all the nine regions of the world right to their limit. Then he climbed up Sumer Mountain where he saw the assembly of Sidhs. There were Gorakh and eighty four other Sidhs who thought of holding a debate with him. The Sidhs asked Guru Nanak Dev Ji: 'O Child! What power has brought you here?' Guru Ji replied that he had meditated on Lord's Name with loving devotion and that power had brought him to that place. And then the Sidh Yogis asked: "O Child! Please tell us your name." Guru Nanak replied that he was Nanak who had achieved emancipation by meditating on the divine name of Lord. And that meditation performed humbly and with love can bring a lowly person to a higher level of existence. 28.*

*Then Sidh Yogis asked Guru Nanak Dev Ji: "What was happening in the mortal world?" From the divine radiance of Guru Nanak's face and his unarguable answers, the Yogis had guessed that he had come for emancipation of the people of Kalyug and therefore must be an incarnation. Guru Nanak Dev Ji replied that falsehood had spread like the darkness of moonless night and he had set out in search of truth in the world. The Earth is in the grip of sins. Righteousness and compassion has disappeared from the face of the Earth and the bull (mythological) of compassion supporting the Earth is wailing under the burden. Sidh Yogis (the realized souls) have hidden themselves in the mountains who should have been guiding the world to the right path. Who else would emancipate the people? The wandering hermits of Yogmat are full of ignorance. Except roaming about with ash-smeared bodies, they have done nothing to allay the existing falsehood. Without the wisdom and guidance of a Guru, the whole world has been drowned in falsehood and perjury. 29.*

*O Master of the Earth! The mentality of human beings in this Kalyug has become dog-like. Flesh of the dead has become its staple diet. (It has become unconcerned about what is right and what is not right). Rulers are sinning. The fence is eating the crop of the field. The subjects are devoid of true knowledge and are thus blind. Other tan falsehood and untruth, they utter nothing else. Disciples are playing the instruments and their teachers (Gurus) are performing various dances to their tunes. The disciples stay put in their homes while their teachers go to them. The Quazis who dispense justice have become corrupt and accept bribes to give decisions in favour of the offenders. Love between a husband and wife has been reduced to the level of monetary gains. It makes no difference where each one of them go and what they do. The whole world is caught in the vice of sin and evil. 30.*

*The Sidhas put their heads together to work out ways how this child (Guru Nanak) could be brought around to accept their Yogmat (Yog Philosophy). 'Such a Yogi would brighten up our cult/ism in this dark age (Kalyug) if he joins us", they thought. Then the head of Yogis gave a cranium to Guru Nanak and asked him to fetch water in it from a nearby pond. Baba (Guru Nanak) got up to fetch water in it. When Baba (Guru Nanak) came to the pond, he found it filled with pearls, rubies and precious stones. The True Guru (Guru Nanak) was a complete Guru-like person and was inaccessible. Who could bear his grandeur, glory and flourish? Babna returned and told the head Yogi that there was no water there. (He turned the illusion of the Nath on him). Guru Ji won over the entre congregation of the Sidhs with his sermons and teachings and thus conveyed the doctrine of his faith that was unique and distinct. Guru Nanak told them that Lord's Name alone was provider of peace and tranquility in Kalyug. 31.*

4. This place is about thirty miles away from Vatala. It has been an old stay of the Yogis, and is now even. Where Guru Ji sat, there is Gurdwara also.

5. Liquor is prepared from jiggery and flowers of basia-latifolia. Yogis used to drink wine.

• The Bani named Sidh Gost is in SGGS. Sidhas did have the discourse, but the composition of question and answers is the creation of Guru Nanak himself. State of affairs at Vatala has been given in more detail by Bhai Gurdas Ji in his Vaars given above.

## Sakhi 51.

1. Bhai Gurdas Jee was a renowned GurSikh, writer, poet and a great Guru-oriented personality during the times of third, fourth, fifth and sixth Gurus. Whatever he has left written regarding the time stands as prior information of the book. As such, giving of the writing here will help the readers to know about those old times as really true ones. In the Sakhi, the writer writes that Guru Jee came from Sumeir to Achal Vatala at the desired speed. But Bhai Gurdas Jee writes that Guru Jee came to Vatala on hearing about the Shivrat fair. Then he (Bhai Gurdas) tells in detail the state of Achal. From there, we come to know that the discourse with Sidhas took place here itself. Moreover, the mistake that the learned ones often commit while explaining about the *Sidh Goast* that 'Guru Jee accompanied Jogis

to have a discussion' gets corrected. Bhai Gurdas Jee clarifies that 'Guru Jee did not go in the group of *Sidhas* to have a discourse – *goast*; rather the *Sidhas* came in the congregation of Guru Jee. The same becomes apparent from the Bani *Sidh Goast*: '*Sidh Sabha Kar Asan Baithe*' (SGGS 938) that the Sidhas sat with proper postures in the congregation.

At the end *Sidh Goast,* Guru Jee tells that the *Sidha* disciples and the *Sidhas* themselves too ask for well-being of 'Naam' ecstasy. So Bhai Gurdas Jee says it means that by leaving the perseverant penance, the *Sidhas* acquired peace and poise by taking up the ideal *sabad simran* of Guru Nanak Dev Jee. It is from Bhai Gurdas Jee only that we come to know that Guru Jee went to Multan after rising from Vatala.

From the Janam Sakhi, we cannot know much as to what extent 'the eulogy of Waheguru' of Guru Nanak had acquired its preaching effect, and what sort of the flow of elixir was running in Kartarpur. This too we come to know from Bhai Gurdas Jee only and, as such, we give here the text of step 32 to step 45 of Vaar One.

*Baba (Guru Nanak) then wore blue clothes (like Muslims) and went to Mecca, the holy place of Muslims. He was the personification pf God in this garb. He carried a long staff in his hand, a book/note book under his armpit and a prayer mat used by the Muslim faithful when offering Namaz. He went and sat in the holy mosque where those who came on Hajj were performing their Hajj rituals. As the night fell, Baba laid down to sleep with his legs and feet extended towards the holt stone (Kaba). A devotee and a religious leader of sort named; Jiwan' kicked Baba with his foot and asked who was that infidel sleeping like a chest and a faithless person. O man! Why are you lying here with your legs extended towards God? Why are you becoming a sinner? Jiwan got hold of Baba's feet and dragged his legs so as to turn them away from the direction of Kaba. Baba showed such divine power so as to turn the holy shrine (Mecca) in the direction his feet were moved to. Bewildered, all present started supplicating before him.32.*

*(Question-Answers with Quaziz and Maulanas). The Quaziz and Mulanas (scholars of Islam) gathered around Baba and started asking questions on matter of religion. God has created a magnificent event and its expanse (of the Universe) is beyond the perception of anyone. They asked Baba to search his book and state who was superior – Hindu or Muslim. Baba told the Hajjis that bereft of good and virtuous deeds both will cry in the court of the Lord. Both the Hindus and Muslims will not entitle them a place in the court of the Lord. To be called a*

*Hindu or a Muslim is like the colour of safflower. It is washed away easily with water. Both are jealous of each other. They slander equally. Thus both followers of Ram (Hindu) and Rahim (Allah) are standing at the same level spiritually.33.*

*Having established his authenticity as a divine person that generated respect in the hearts of Hajjis to the extent of worship, Baba left a memento of wooden slippers that he wore during his sojourn there. Wherever Baba went, he showered his precepts to the people and allayed their doubts thus liberating them from repeated births. Baba was revered in every home regardless whether it was a Hindu or Muslim household. When the sun rose, brightness prevailed all around. Now it cannot be hidden by anyone. And when the lion roared in the jungle, the herd of deeds ran helter-skelter. Once the moon is out and its light spreads, it cannot be hidden howsoever one may try concealing and covering it with four kneading basin. From East to the West he had the whole world won over by his divine traits. He had the Lord's command implemented in the whole world.34.*

*Then Baba went to Baghdad and camped outside the city. On one hand, Baba was an epitome of Timeless Lord; while on the other hand, he had the company of Mardana, the rebeck player. Worshipping the Lord in his unique style, he proclaimed loudly that Lord's name is eternal. This loud proclamation mesmerized the entire city. The entire city of Bagdad fell silent and dumb. Its principal Pir (the reigning Muslim saint) was amazed. He contemplated and focused his mind to know who had come to the city? He realized that a carefree faquir who has no other desire than to meet the Lord and is absorbed in divine love of the Lord had camped just outside the city. Dastgir, the Pir of Bagdad, came and asked Baba who he was and what cult/ sect he belonged to? Mardana replied: 'Nanak is his name. He has come in the Kalyug in the garb of God. His sect/cult is that of God. He is known both on the earth and sky beside all the four directions of the world. 35.*

*Pir Dastgir did not take this intrusion too kindly. He felt agitated and let out his anger by putting numerous questions to Guru Nanak. He was convinced that he (Baba Nanak) was a hermit blessed with divine powers. Here in Baghdad he had shown much prowess. "He (Guru Nanak) says that there are millions of Universes and galaxies. That indeed is an amazing statement made by him." Dastgir asked him that he too would like to see all this expanse of nature that he has seen. So he requested Guru Nanak to use his power and show him all that he has seen. Baba held the hand of a young son of Pir Dastgir and asked him to close his eyes.*

Both Baba and he were space bound in no time. In a time taken for a wink, the young son of Dastgir was shown countless skies and nether regions. And when they returned from their long voyage of space, the young son of Pir Dastgir had a bowl of Karah Parshad (consecrated food) that he brought from the divine abode. The manifested divine power of Guru Nanak became apparent. 36. Having subjugated Mecca and Medina, Baba had now humbled the city of Baghdad, a strong hold of Islam. He won over the eighty four sects of Sidh Yogis and hypocrisies of six schools of Indian philosophy. Beside numerous universes and galaxies, he established his authority as spiritual teacher of the world. He conquered the nine regions of the Earth and spread the authority of SatNam, One who is eternal. All the gods, demons, monsters and the deity maintaining record of deeds of everyone in the divine court fell at his feet. Even god Indra and the beautiful fairy singers of his court sing invocatory songs in praise of Guru Nanak. The world was filled with joy when Guru Nanak came to liberate the people of Kalyuga. He made both Hindus and Muslims humble. 37.

Then Baba came to Kartarpur. He shed his as a recluse. He started wearing clothes of worldly people, made himself available to all for help and advice. By establishing Guru Angad in his place, he made the tradition run unconventionally. His sons did not respect and honour his teachings. They became rebellious and base of mind. They started keeping themselves away from him. Guru Nanak now started uttering his compositions so that its radiance would destroy the darkness of ignorance. Spiritual discussions and exchange of views commenced among the holy men at Kartarpur. The atmosphere so developed resulted in perpetual sounding of the unstruck music in the consciousness of the listeners. A set routine followed at Kartarpur. Jap(u) Bani was recited in the morning while So-dar and Arti were sung in the evening. Guru-conscious Sikhs discarded the teachings of Atharv Veda and reposed their faith in Guru's utterances. 38.

Hearing about Shivratri fair, Baba came to Achal Vatala. The whole world thronged the place for his glimpse. Money in the form of offerings started pouring in as if all divine gains were falling at his feet. The Yogis were angry and jealous of Guru Nanak at this wondrous development. Some devotees were entertaining by enacting scenes depicting early life of Lord Krishna. Pleased, the spectators would drop a few coins in the pot placed by the artists for the purpose. Angered at being ignored, the Yogis hid their pot of coins with their mystical powers. Finding their pot of coins missing, the players forgot about their act. They were more concerned in finding the missing pot since it had all their earnings. Baba being a clairvoyant and knower of *hearts knew where the pot had been hidden. He took out the pot from its hiding and handed it over to the performers. That made the Yogis more angry and envious. 39.*

*Envious and peeved at the development, all the Yogis got together and decided to hold a dialogue/discussion with Guru Nanak. So they came over to him. Then Yogi Bhangar Nath asked Baba Ji why he had put citrus extract in the milk pot. The milk had split and any amount of churning would not produce the butter. Having renounced the world, why had he become a householder again? Nanak replied to Bhangar Nath that his wisdom was misplaced and not channelized in right direction. You have not put the milk in a clean vessel like heart. Through erroneous love of the guise, you have ruined the milk. Having become a recluse and divorced from family life, you still go to the householders to beg for food. And yet you go and slander them. You should know that one cannot get anything without giving. 40.*

*Hearing these words, the Yogis flew into rage. They shrieked and shouted and changed their forms into demons, monsters and ghosts. They then said that Nanak, a person of Bedi lineage who took birth in Kalyug has condemned/rejected the six schools of Hindu philosophy. The Sidh Yogis were singing out Tantric incantations as remedy of all that Nanak had done to them. Some of them changed their form into lion and wolf and displayed many miracles. One Yogi wore wings and started flying just like a bird who floats in the air. One changed himself into a snake and started hissing while the other started causing rainfall of embers. Bhangar Nath started plucking stars while someone else climbed up a deer skin and started floating on water. The fire of hatred and jealousy in the hearts of Sidhs would just not be put off with all these stunts. 41.*

*'Listen, O Nanak! What miracle you have shown to the world?' said the Sidhs. 'Show us something similar. Why have you taken so long?' "Nath Ji! said Baba (Guru Nanak). 'I have seen the Yogis and I find them not worthy of anything." And to me, other than holy congregation of God-loving people and Guru's utterances, I have no other support. The Creator is benedict and blissful. Guru Nanak remained steadfast just as the Earth remains firm on its place. Sidh Yogis used all their charms and incantations. The divine words of Guru rendered all their skill ineffective. Guru himself is donor and granter of boons. No one has ever been able to evaluate his capabilities. And then becoming humble, they fell at the holy feet of Guru Nanak. 42.*

*Baba then addressed the Yogis and said, "O Nath Ji! Listen to the divine word. I am telling you the truth. "Except the miraculous True Name of the Lord that I enshrine in my heart, I have no other miracle with me. Even if I wear clothes of fire, or I go and live in Himalayas in the house made of snow; and I prepare dishes of iron, have the Earth have tied and drive it like an animal. Exercise so much power and authority that the whole Earth keeps moving ahead of me like a herd of animals. So much so that I become capable of weighing the entire Earth and sky with just a small weights of 65 grams (nearly a chhatank according to Indian weights and measures); I should have so much power in me that that I am able to get whatever I want done by anybody." All this is no more than shadow of a cloud against the power of Lord's Word SatNam."43.*

*Baba had discussion with Sidh Yogis and that brought peace and calmness to their mind. His words soothed them all and they felt tranquil and serene. Baba Nanak had won over the entire fair of Shivratri. Those who held faith on the six schools of Hindu philosophy now bowed before him with reverence. All the Sidh Yogis were full of praise for him and said in one voice: "O Nanak, your achievements are great and praiseworthy. You are a great man who has lit the lamp of knowledge and Nam Simran in Kalyug." Baba decamped from the fair at Achal Vatala and headed towards Multan. Multan was a center Muslim pirs who had become very arrogant and haughty. Seeing the arrival of Baba Nanak there, they brought a wide based bowl of milk full to the brim. Baba plucked a Jasmine from a bush by his side and placed it on the surface of the milk. It was the river Ganges merging in the ocean. 44.*

*The reputation of his spiritual skill started spreading with every passing day. He made people meditate on the Name of the Lord. And he taught them that asking God for grant of worldly boons instead of divine Name is asking for distresses. Guru Nanak spread the doctrine of obeying divine command and thus he laid foundation of a religion free of the dross if ego. In his life-time itself, he installed Baba Lehna (Guru Angad Dev Ji) on the seat of Guru in his place and had the canopy of reverence adorning over his head. Merging his light eternal with that of Baba Lehna Ji, it seemed Guru Nanak had only changed his form original to that of Baba Lehna. Nobody could access this mystery because a quaint had been caused within an astonishment. Guru Nanak changed the form of (Guru) Angad just as he himself was. 45.*

2. When Guru Nanak Dev Ji reached Mecca, then the Pir Supreme Makhdum, Seikh Ibrahim of Patna, and Dastgir and one or two more Hindustani Faqirs were there. They had their discourse with Guru Ji there. Pir Patlia too could have been among them. The word 'Patnia' could refer to Pir Seikh Ibrahim Farid Sani

of Pak Pattan. Bhai Sahib Sangat Singh came to know about this from the dynastic Pirs there on reaching 'Uch'. He told that the 'wooden wear' that Guru Nanak Dev Ji had given there were brought by asking from there by our ancestors, and the same have been kept respectfully with us. The aspect needs more research in this regard.

3. Ahead is the sIhr&I as given in Appendix 5. It is not in SGGS, and neither is it real one because the conversation with Rukandin was held not in Punjabi. That was in Persian or Arabic.

4. This *sabad* is by Bhagat Kabir. The writer, by mistake, has put it 'Mehla 1'.

# Sakhi 52.

• As already given, Bhai Gurdas has confirmed that the Sidh Gost took place at Achal Vatala. Writing about Gorakh Hattri is wrong by the writer.

• The *sabad* actually is by the Fifth Guru.

# Sakhi 53

• The version relates to previous period of Guru Ji's life when people used to call him 'crazy'. Presently in Kartarpur, he has been acknowledged as worldly worshipped being and people from far and wide come to pay obeisance before him. Alittle later, Gorakh says: 'bhuq pswrw kIqo hI' – a lot of expansion has been made, and that shows that Guru Ji's spiritual magnificence had flourished a lot.

# Sakhi 55.

1. Sri Guru Nanak Dev Ji now lives at Kartarpur. He has been in Talwandi when he was in childhood or in young age. This is the writer's lapse.

# Sakhi 56.

1. This *sabad* is of the Fifth Guru. It is wrong on the writer's part.

# Sakhi 57.

The writing as written on the last page refers to writing of the Sakhi after the Tenth Master i.e. after 1699 AD, when Khalsa was installed. Or the line seems to have been written by the writer himself after copying the matter, since this epithet came into use at the time of serving Amrit in 1699 AD.

## Publisher's Note

We are Grateful to Bhai Vir Singh ji foundation for giving us this opportunity to translate his work into English so it can reach a much wider audience worldwide.

We are thankful to Khanuja family foundation of Phoenix for sharing the photographs from their collection in this book. We are also thankful to Mike Lundgren for taking the Photographs.

We are thankful to Prof. Jogi for undertaking this difficult task and translating this important work into English.

We are thankful to Gurmeet Singh Sandhu of Ottawa, Canada for his dedicated and altruistic effort in editing and rephrasing the story sections along with the narrations of Sakhis.

The expenses to bring this important work to print were possible due to funding from a Non Profit Sikh Love Organization of Phoenix, Arizona, USA. Proceeds from the sale of this book will used to fund more such projects in future. We will also provide this book free of charge to universities and libraries both in India and abroad.

Lastly we are grateful to Amazon book services for publishing the book.

Sikh Love Organization,

Phoenix, Arizona, USA.

Contact: web; Sikhlove.org or via Facebook page.

Guru Nanak Ji with Mardana and Bala, C 1785

Guru Nanak Ji with Bala, C 1790-1820

Guru Nanak Ji at Mecca, Late 18th C

Guru Nanak Ji as Shopkeeper, Late 19th C

Guru Nanak Ji with Brahmin, Early 19th C